KT-591-974

Contents

		page
Introduction		v
Chapter 1	The Black Case	1
Chapter 2	Job Hunting	5
Chapter 3	The Fire	10
Chapter 4	A Trip to the Hospital	16
Chapter 5	Meeting Kelly	21
Chapter 6	The Exam	26
Chapter 7	Donny Ray's Statement	33
Chapter 8	Surprises For Drummond	42
Chapter 9	The Funeral	49
Chapter 10	An Important Discovery	55
Chapter 11	Choosing a Jury	58
Chapter 12	The Trial	62
Chapter 13	The Verdict	72
Chapter 14	The Last Beating	77
Chapter 15	Winners and Losers	81
Activities		87

Introduction

I have no job. I have no money. I have debts I can't pay.
I do, however, have a case. And it may be a very good one.

Rudy Baylor is ready to finish law school and start his first real job with a big law firm when his life begins to change very quickly. First, he loses the job that was going to provide him with a good salary. And second, Dot and Bud Black need his help in fighting a big insurance company. Their son, Donny Ray, is dying, and his claim for medical treatment that could save his life has been refused. Can an inexperienced student really give them any hope? How will Rudy live while he fights the case for his poor clients? And who is the attractive married woman that Rudy cannot get out of his mind?

John Grisham, one of the world's most popular authors, was born in Arkansas, USA, in 1955. After graduating from college in 1981, he became a lawyer and was also involved in politics. When his first two books, *A Time to Kill* and *The Firm,* made him famous, though, Grisham was able to give up the law and become a full-time writer. His other books include *The Pelican Brief, The Client, The Chamber, The Runaway Jury, The Partner* and *The Street Lawyer,* and many of them have also become movies. *The Rainmaker* stars Matt Damon, Claire Danes, Jon Voight and Mary Kay Place, with Mickey Rourke and Danny DeVito.

John Grisham lives with his family in Virginia and Mississippi.

Chapter 1 The Black Case

It's no secret that there are too many lawyers here in Memphis. Next month, when we graduate from law school, many graduates won't have jobs to go to. Some of those who do have jobs will be doing boring work for very little money. The lucky ones, who have been accepted by big private firms, will work seventy hours a week but will make real money.

I am one of the lucky ones. I have a job in a small, respectable firm called Brodnax and Speer, and I'll be making more money than I can spend.

At least that's what I thought until a few minutes ago. I just heard that Brodnax and Speer has been bought by Tinley Britt, one of the big old firms. I called but no one would tell me anything. I'm driving my old Toyota as calmly as I can and wondering whether I still have a job.

I walk into the building. Richard Spain, a really nice guy who took me to lunch the first time I visited here, is sitting by the elevators, looking at the floor.

"Richard, it's me, Rudy Baylor." Richard doesn't move. I sit down next to him. "What's the matter, Richard?" I ask.

"They fired me. They fired all of us. Tinley Britt just wanted our clients. You're fired, too, Rudy. Do you realize you lost your first job before you even started?"

I take the elevator to the fourth floor.

"And who are you?" asks the uniformed guard at the desk.

"Rudy Baylor."

"Here, this is for you. Read it and leave."

It is one paragraph. I have no job. I have no money.

I do, however, have a case. And it may be a very good one.

◆

1

One of my classes this year is Legal Problems of the Elderly. To get experience we visit a club for elderly people and give them free legal advice. We went today.

It seems like weeks have passed since Dot Black came up to me with the papers, but it was only this morning. She and her husband are younger than the others.

"Buddy and me, we don't have much money," she says quietly, embarrassed. "And we need a lawyer," she adds.

"What's the problem?" I ask.

"We're being cheated by an insurance company. We started a medical policy five years ago when our two sons were seventeen. We've never missed a payment. My boy Donny Ray got leukemia eight months ago, and now he's dying because Great Benefit won't pay for a bone marrow transplant."

"A transplant?" I say, confused.

"My boys are identical twins. Bone marrow from Donny Ray's brother, Ron, is a perfect match for Donny Ray's – the doctors said so. The transplant costs about $150,000. The insurance company is supposed to pay it – it says so in the policy. So Donny Ray is dying because of them." Dot pushes a pile of papers across the desk.

I look quickly through the papers: the policy and letters to and from Great Benefit.

"Are you *sure* bone marrow transplants are covered in the policy?" I ask.

"Hell, yes. Our doctor said they should pay because bone marrow transplants are routine treatment now."

I look at the next letter. At first it looks like all the others, quick and nasty.

Dear Mrs. Black:

On seven previous occasions, this company has denied your claim in writing. We now deny it for the eighth and final time. You must be stupid, stupid, stupid!

It was signed by the head of the claims department. I can't believe it.

"I'll have to study these," I say. "Can you send me his medical records?"

"Sure, but please hurry, Rudy. My boy is dying."

I go home and read everything Dot gave me. I read the Stupid Letter again. It is shocking and mean and written by someone who never thought the Blacks would show it to a lawyer.

I study the records. The Blacks paid $18.00 a week for five years. I keep thinking about Max Leuberg, who taught Insurance Law last fall. I'm not a real lawyer but this is a real case and I need help.

◆

I find Leuberg's office in the Law School. It's filled with books and newspapers and files. It's a mess.

"Come in," he shouts. He's a thin, short man, sixty with wild hair and hands that are always moving. He wears jeans and a T-shirt. "Baker! What can I do for you?"

"Baylor, Rudy Baylor," I say. Then I tell him about the Blacks' fight with Great Benefit. He listens to every word. "Have you ever heard of Great Benefit?"

"Yeah. It's a big company that sells a lot of cheap insurance. Very unpleasant. Let me see the policy. What are their reasons for refusing to pay?"

"First they just refused. Then they said leukemia wasn't covered. Then that Donny Ray had leukemia before they bought the policy. Then that he was an adult and wasn't covered by his parents' policy."

"Were all the premiums paid?"

"Mrs. Black says they were," I answer.

"The bastards," says Max, smiling. Max loves this kind of fight, poor people against big, powerful companies. "And you've checked the whole file?"

"Yeah, I read everything the client gave me," I say. I give him the Stupid Letter. He reads it twice.

"Unbelievable," he says. "I'll read it all tonight."

"No problem," I say. "Can I come back tomorrow?"

"Sure. Anytime." I'll meet him, listen to his advice and then type up a two-page report for the Blacks.

◆

All through Law School I've worked nights at Yogi's Bar. It's a student place, owned by Prince Thomas. Prince is a big man with thick arms and long hair. He likes to sit at a table near the big screen TV, watch the ball games, talk to pretty girls and drink.

People say that not all Prince's business activities are exactly legal, but I don't care. He's been good to me. For twenty hours a week I make five dollars an hour. Every day students come in looking for work, so I feel lucky to have the job.

It's OK to be a waiter while you're a student, but it won't be OK when I graduate. I have to find a real job.

First I try the Law School Employment Office, Madeline Skinner. She's very good at what she does. She knows the right people in the right firms because she helped them get their jobs when they left college.

"Hello, Rudy."

"Hi," I say, smiling.

"Rough day, huh?" She knows. "Brodnax and Spear wanted to keep you but the new firm refused," she says.

"So what's left?" I ask.

"Not much," she says quickly. "In fact, nothing."

"What should I do?"

"Start knocking on doors. There are three thousand lawyers in this city, mostly people working alone or in small firms. Offer to do the work they don't want."

"How many times have you given this advice lately?"

"We have fifteen graduates looking for work."

"Thanks, Mrs. Skinner."

"I'll keep looking. Check with me next week."

I go to the library. Booker Kane is waiting to study for the bar with me. Booker is black and my best friend. He and his wife Charlene have invited me to dinner twice a month for three years.

"Booker, I've lost the job at Brodnax and Spear."

He looks shocked. "So what are you going to do?"

"Find another job. Study." I tell him about the Black case. "Max Leuberg is reading the stuff tonight."

Chapter 2   Job Hunting

When I get to Max Leuberg's office, he smiles. "I read the whole file last night. This kind of behavior is typical of these companies. They sell to the uneducated and when claims are made the companies refuse to pay."

"Don't they get sued?"

"Not often. Their clients are the kind of people who are afraid of lawyers and the legal system."

"What happens when they *do* get sued?" I ask.

"Generally, not much. There have been some large settlements around the country."

"But Donny Ray is dying because he can't get the transplant he's supposed to get under the policy, right?"

"Yes, if his parents have told you everything, it's a good case. Not a great one. This is Tennessee, where there are rarely large settlements – especially in Memphis."

"So what do I do?" I ask.

"Sue the bastards."

"I don't have a license."

"Not you. Send the family to an experienced lawyer. Make a few phone calls for them. Do what you can."

"Thanks," I say.

♦

The Black home is a small brick house, like a thousand others in the neighborhood except that the front yard is neater than most. An old Chevrolet sits in the garage.

It's mid-afternoon and the temperature is nearly ninety. The windows and doors are open. I knock gently and Dot comes to the front door.

"It's me, Mrs. Black. Rudy Baylor. I'd like to discuss a few things." I follow her into the kitchen. Buddy isn't around, and I guess Donny Ray is in his bedroom.

"Where's Buddy?" I ask, like we are old friends.

She points out the window to the back yard. Under a tree is an old Ford Fairlane. It's white with two doors, both of which are open. A cat is sleeping on the roof.

"He's sitting in his car," she explains.

The car looks like it hasn't moved in a long time.

"Where's he going?" I ask, and she actually smiles.

"Buddy, he ain't going nowhere. He sits in there every day, all day, just Buddy and the cats. Buddy ain't right in the head."

"How's Donny Ray?" I ask.

"He stays in bed most of the time."

"Look, I advise you to sue immediately. But don't expect a quick solution. You're fighting a big company with lots of lawyers who can delay and delay."

"How long will it take?"

"It could take months, maybe years."

"He'll be dead in a few months."

"Can I ask you something? Great Benefit first denied this

claim last August, right after Donny Ray was diagnosed. Why did you wait until now to see a lawyer?"

"I thought the insurance company would pay the claim. I kept writing them, they kept writing back. I don't know. Just stupid, I guess. We'd paid the premiums so regularly over the years, never late. And, I ain't never used a lawyer, you know. No divorce or anything like that ..." She turns sadly and looks through the window at the Fairlane. "He drinks a lot, you know. And I don't really care. It makes him happy."

"Look, Dot, I know I don't have any experience but I'd like to handle this case for you." She has an almost hopeless look on her face. One lawyer's as good as the next. How strange. Lawyers spend a fortune on advertising, but there are still people like Dot who don't know an experienced lawyer from a third-year law student. "I'll have to work with another lawyer, until I pass the bar exam, you know."

"How much will it cost?" she asks, looking at me.

I give her a smile. "Nothing. I'll take a third of whatever we get. If we don't win, I don't get anything."

"How much?"

"We sue for millions," I say, and she smiles. I don't think there is a greedy bone in this woman's body. Any dreams she had disappeared long ago. But she likes the idea of making Great Benefit suffer.

"And you get a third of it?"

"Yes. After Donny Ray's medical bills are paid."

She hits the table. "Then do it. Now, OK?"

"I'll start work," I say.

"Don't you want to meet Donny Ray?"

"I'll come back soon to ask him a few questions."

"Just hurry, OK?"

◆

7

At Yogi's, I stay busy. Prince is drinking with his lawyer, Bruiser Stone, an enormously fat man with long, thick gray hair and a small beard. Together they look like two bears.

♦

The next day, I have an appointment with Barry X. Lancaster, a rising star in the Lake firm.

Jonathan Lake is famous in Memphis. He graduated from law school and couldn't find a job, so he started in business by himself. One night he crashed his motorcycle and woke up with a broken leg in St. Peter's Hospital.

The guy in the next bed had also had an accident and was badly burned. His girlfriend had died. After he and Lake became friends, Lake signed up both cases, sued, and won.

Six months after passing the bar exam, Jonathan Lake settled the cases for 2.6 million dollars cash. Lake got half. With 1.3 million dollars, Lake built an office and filled it with people. He studied hard, trained himself and quickly became the best trial lawyer in Tennessee.

Barry's quite busy. "Tell me about your case."

"Well, I'm actually here looking for a job," I say boldly. "I saw your advertisement for an assistant."

"I'm really busy."

"OK then," I say. I rush through my usual routine about being bright and in the top third of my class, and how I had a job with Brodnax and Speer. I tell him how useful I can be to him. He can use me to do all his boring work, and pay me twenty-four thousand dollars instead of the usual forty.

"Twenty-one thousand."

"I'll take it," I reply quickly. "I'll work a whole year at twenty-one. I promise I won't leave for twelve months. I'll work sixty, seventy hours a week. No vacation."

"I'll discuss it with Mr. Lake. Maybe he'll agree."

"I also have a very good case." I hand him my report on the Black case, and he reads it twice.

"You want a job and part of the fee?" he asks.

"No, just the job. The case is yours. I'd like to work on it and handle the client, but the fee is yours."

"I'll let you know."

Back at my apartment, the phone rings. It's Barry X. "I'll hire you as an assistant for twelve months. We will represent the Blacks against Great Benefit. You will work on the case but you will not receive any of the fees."

"When do I start?"

"Right now. I'd like to discuss the case tonight. We need to get a contract signed by the Blacks," he says.

◆

I leave Barry's office after ten o'clock. I'm smiling as I drive home. I'll call Booker first thing in the morning with the good news. Then I'll take Mrs. Skinner some flowers.

At Yogi's, Prince says that he is sorry I'm leaving, but I will still work weekends until I take the bar exam.

◆

On my fourth day at Lake's, Barry hands me a thin file.

"I want you to go see the Blacks and get this contract signed by all three. It needs to be done now."

I call Dot and explain. When I arrive, Dot is alone in the kitchen. "Buddy won't come in."

"Why not?" I ask.

Dot just looks out the window. "I'll get Donny Ray."

I hear Dot speaking softly to her son, then they're in the kitchen. I stand to meet Donny Ray Black.

He is definitely close to death, but he smiles and holds out a bony hand, which I shake carefully. "Nice to meet you."

"Mom's said nice things about you," he replies. His voice is weak but his words are clear. "She says you're suing those bastards at Great Benefit."

"That's right," I say.

"Is Daddy coming in?" Donny Ray asks.

"He said he won't," says Dot, sadly.

I pull the contract from the file. "This must be signed by all three of you before we can start suing them."

"Well, he said he ain't coming in," she said.

"Just get a pen and go out there and make him sign the thing," Donny Ray tells his mother angrily.

She walks out slowly across the yard. A cat sees her coming and dives under the car. The doors are open and Dot pushes the contract inside.

"I know you think they're crazy," Donny Ray says, reading my mind. "But they're good people who have had some bad luck. If I'd had the transplant, hell, even six months ago, then I'd have had a 90 percent chance of being cured. Whatever you get out of this case, please take care of them with it."

I hate Great Benefit Life Insurance Company.

Dot opens the door and slides the contract across the table. Buddy has signed it. Donny Ray and his mother sign.

When I leave them, Dot is gently rubbing Donny Ray's arm and telling him that things will get better.

Chapter 3   The Fire

After dark on Tuesday, I'm in my apartment when the phone rings. It's Dot Black, and I know something is wrong because she wouldn't normally call me.

"I just got a phone call," she says, "from a Mr. Barry Lancaster. Said he was my lawyer."

"That's true, Dot. He's an important lawyer with my firm. He works with me."

"Well, that ain't what he said. He called to see if me and Donny Ray can come down to his office tomorrow – he needed to get some things signed. I asked about you, and he said you ain't working there."

I suddenly feel sick. "It's a big firm, and I'm new. He probably just forgot about me."

"No. He said you used to work there, but not now. This is pretty confusing, you know?"

I know. I fall into a chair and try and think clearly. It's almost nine o'clock. "Look, Dot, let me call Mr. Lancaster and find out what's happening. I'll call you back."

I'm friendly. "Barry, Rudy. Did you see my report?"

"Yeah, it looks great." He sounds tired. "Rudy, there's a problem. Jonathan Lake doesn't want to employ you."

"I want to talk to Jonathan Lake," I say, as firmly as possible.

"Absolutely not. He's too busy."

"You bastard."

"Calm down, Rudy."

"Is Lake in the office now?" I demand.

"Probably, but he won't see you."

Ten minutes later I bang on the front door, but nobody appears. A uniformed guard steps from the shadows and holds my shoulder. My knees are weak with fear. He's at least six foot six, black with a black cap.

"You need to leave, son," he says gently in a deep voice.

I push his hand off my shoulder and walk away.

I sit for hours on the old sofa in my apartment. I curse and I cry and then I start to plan my revenge. I finally fall asleep on the sofa, but something wakes me after nine. There are two policemen at the door, and I invite them in.

"Now what's going on?" I ask.

"You know where Jonathan Lake's office is?"

"Yes."

"Did you go there last night?"

"Yes."

"What time?"

"Between nine and ten."

"What was your purpose in going there?"

"It's a long story."

"We have hours."

"I wanted to talk to Jonathan Lake."

"Did you?"

"No. The doors were locked. I couldn't get in."

"Did you try to break in?"

"No."

"Are you sure?"

"Yes. Ask the guard."

The policemen looked at each other. "Can you describe him?"

"Big black guy, probably six-six. Uniform, cap, gun. Ask him – he'll tell you I left when he told me to leave."

"We can't ask him."

"Why not?" I ask. Something awful is coming.

"Because he's dead." They are both watching me carefully to see how I react. I am shocked, like anyone else would be.

"How, uh, how did he die?"

"Burned up in the fire."

"What fire?"

"Someone thinks they saw your car near the office at two this morning."

"Not my car. What fire?" I ask again.

"The Lake firm was burned last night. Completely destroyed."

"And Barry Lancaster told you that I'd make a wonderful suspect," I say.

12

"Mr. Lancaster said you were pretty upset when you went to the office last night."

"True. But not mad enough to set fire to the place. You guys are wasting your time, I swear."

"He said you'd just been fired, and you wanted to talk to Mr. Lake."

"True, true, true. But that doesn't mean that I wanted to burn his offices down."

"You'd better talk to a lawyer. Right now you're the main suspect."

◆

I find Prince in his office at Yogi's. He is not a morning person and I usually try to avoid him until he's had his third drink. That's at about 6 p.m., so I'm much too early.

"What's wrong?" he says. His eyes are red, he looks terrible and he's in a bad mood.

"I'm in trouble," I say. I tell him about losing the job, the fire, the police, the dead body, everything.

"So Lake got burned down." He looks amused. "I never particularly liked him. You sure you didn't do it?"

"Of course not, Prince."

"You'd better talk to a lawyer."

"I can't afford a lawyer," I say.

"Let me call Bruiser." He picks up the phone and a few minutes later we're in the back of Prince's Cadillac and he's telling me all about his old friend's career. Oddly, I begin to relax.

Bruiser went to law school at night and finished when he was twenty-two. He and Prince were best friends as children, and in high school. When Bruiser went to college, Prince bought a beer truck. They could write a book about the things they've done together since then.

I've served Bruiser a thousand drinks but I've never had an

actual conversation with him. I explain my problem.

"I saw it on the news. When do you take the bar exam?"

"July."

"Then what?"

"I don't know. I'll look around."

Prince jumps into the conversation. "Can't you use him around here, Bruiser? You have a lot of lawyers – what difference does one more make? He's a top student, bright, works hard."

I look at Prince, who smiles at me like Santa Claus. We both look at Bruiser, who's trying to think of an excuse. "Uh, sure. I'm always looking for good legal talent, but it wouldn't exactly be a salaried position. I expect people to pay for themselves."

"How does that work?" I ask.

"You get a thousand dollars a month and you keep one third of the fees you earn. One third goes to my office, for secretarial work. One third comes to me. If your third is less than a thousand, you owe me the difference." Bruiser is watching me closely. He's offering me the only job left in the city of Memphis, and he knows I don't want to take it.

"When can I start?"

"Right now."

"But the bar exam . . ."

"Don't worry about it." He hands me a ring with two keys on it. "You're free to come and go at all hours. Be careful at night. This is not the best part of town."

"There's something else." I give him a rapid, fact-filled report on the Black case and explain how Barry Lancaster used me so he could steal the case. "We have to file suit today, because Lancaster technically owns the case. I think he'll file soon."

"Have the clients signed up with Lake?"

"Yes, but I'm going to go see them now. They'll listen to me." I show Bruiser a copy of the lawsuit against Great Benefit and a letter that I've typed to Barry X. Lancaster, to be signed by all the

Blacks, closing their contract with Lake. He reads them slowly.

"This is good work, Rudy. Let me guess – you file the lawsuit this afternoon, show a copy to the Blacks, then ask them to sign the letter."

"Right. I just need your name and signature on the lawsuit. I'll do all the work and keep you informed."

"I like it. What's the lawsuit worth?"

"Probably whatever the jury says."

"And you're going to be the trial lawyer?"

"I'll need a little help. It's about a year or two away."

"I'll introduce you to Deck Shifflet. He used to work for a big insurance company and checks a lot of policies for me. His office is down the hall from yours. Get this document rewritten, put my name on it, and we'll get it filed today. Just make sure that the clients agree."

"They will. Thanks," I say.

◆

Five minutes before the court's offices close, I file my lawsuit against Great Benefit Life Insurance. My clients, the Blacks, are asking for two hundred thousand dollars actual damages plus ten million dollars in punitive damages. I pulled the figure of ten million from the air because it sounds good. Trial lawyers do this all the time. Great Benefit has officially been sued!

I race across town to my client. Buddy is outside, but Dot fetches Donny Ray from his room and the three of us sit around the table while they admire their copy of the lawsuit and the big numbers. Dot keeps repeating the sum of ten million.

I explain what happened with those awful people at the Lake firm, but Dot and Donny Ray really don't care. The lawsuit has been filed, and they can read it as often as they want. They want to know what happens next and what the chances are of a quick settlement. These questions are difficult. I know the process will

15

take too long, and I feel cruel hiding this.

I persuade them to sign a letter firing Barry X. Lancaster, and a new contract with the firm of J. Lyman Stone. I explain the new paperwork. Donny Ray and I watch as Dot quarrels with her husband out in the car.

They're more cheerful now. They've finally fought back and sued this company that they hate.

♦

But I've got other problems. I have no idea how Bruiser expects me to start making money immediately. If I win the Black case, it'll be many months away. I'll continue at Yogi's for a while – five dollars an hour, dinner, and a few beers.

Firms in this town usually expect their lawyers to wear nice suits, drive a good car, live in a respectable house, even to spend time at the right clubs. Not my firm. I can wear anything, go anywhere, and no one cares.

Suddenly, I have a wonderful feeling of independence. I'm going to be OK!

I need to tell Booker about my recent adventures. For three years we've been able to encourage and help each other. Now we've got to get back to studying. The bar exam is very close.

Chapter 4   A Trip to the Hospital

I'm in my office, wondering how I'm supposed to make a thousand dollars this month, when Bruiser comes in. He slides a piece of paper across my desk.

"It's a copy of a police report," he says, already halfway to the door.

"About me?" I ask, suddenly frightened.

"No, it's an accident report! A car wreck last night. Maybe a drunk driver who drove through a red light."

"Do we represent one of the—"

"Not yet! It's your job to get the case. Find out everything you can. There might be some good injuries."

I'm thoroughly confused, and he leaves me that way.

The accident report is filled with information: names of drivers and passengers, addresses, telephone numbers, injuries, damage to vehicles, witness reports. Both drivers were taken to the hospital. The one who drove through the red light *had* been drinking. What do I do now?

My door opens slowly and a thin little man puts his head in. "Rudy? I'm Deck Shifflet," he says without a smile. "Bruiser said you had a case you wanted to talk about."

"Nice to meet you." Deck could be forty or fifty. Most of his hair is gone, and he wears glasses that are quite thick and dirty. It's difficult to tell if his head is extra large or his body is small, but the two don't fit. Poor Deck is one of the ugliest men I've ever seen.

"Yes," I say. "It's an insurance case. Are you one of the lawyers here?"

"Not really. I've been to law school, but I haven't passed the bar exam."

Ah, just like me. "Oh, really," I say. "When did you finish law school?"

"Five years ago. You see, I'm having a little trouble with the exam. I've tried five times."

"Sorry to hear it."

"When do *you* take it?" he asks, nervously.

"July. It's difficult, isn't it?"

"Yeah. I haven't taken it in a year. I don't know if I'll ever try again."

"Yeah, well, how long have you worked for Bruiser?"

"Three years. He treats me like everyone else. I find the cases, work on them, give him his money. Everybody's happy."

I hand the accident report to him, and he reads it quickly. "Bruiser gave it to you, right?"

"Yeah. What does he expect me to do?"

"Find the guy who got hit. Make him your client."

"How do I find him?"

"Well, he's probably still in the hospital. That's usually the best place to find them."

"You go to the hospitals?"

"Sure, all the time. Bruiser has some contacts in the police department. They send him these accident reports almost every morning. He gives them out around the office, and he expects us to go get the cases."

"Which hospital?"

"What did they teach you in law school?"

"Well, they didn't teach us to chase ambulances."

"Then you'd better learn quickly or you'll get pretty hungry. Call the home phone number, tell whoever answers that you're with the Memphis Fire Department and you need to speak to the injured driver. He can't come to the phone because he's in the hospital. You ask which one."

I feel sick. "Then what?"

"Look, you're new. Let's go and find this boy."

I really don't want to. I'd like to walk out of this place and never come back. But at the moment I have nothing else to do. "OK," I say.

He jumps to his feet. "Meet me outside. I'll call and find out which hospital."

♦

At St. Peter's Hospital Deck leads me straight to the information desk. Within seconds he has the room number of Dan Van Landel, our possible client.

"Don't act like a lawyer," he whispers. Deck, sadly, has done this many times.

Van Landel is in his late twenties. One eye is swollen almost completely shut, the other has a cut under it. An arm is broken, a leg is very badly injured and raised above the bed. His jaw is wired shut.

"Good afternoon, Mr. Van Landel. Can you hear me?"

"Who are you?" he asks through his teeth.

"Deck Shifflet, from the law firm of Lyman Stone," he says, with complete confidence. "You haven't talked to an insurance company, have you?" Just like that, Deck shows who the bad guys are. Not us.

"No," says Van Landel.

"Good, don't talk to them. They just want to cheat you," Deck says, already giving advice. "We've looked at the accident report – a clear case of driving through a red light. We're going out there to photograph the area, talk to witnesses. We have to do it quickly before the insurance company gets to the witnesses. Sometimes they even offer them money to lie in court. We need to move fast. Do you have a lawyer?"

I hold my breath.

"No," he says.

"Well, my firm handles more car wrecks than anybody in Memphis, and we get very large settlements. Insurance companies are afraid of us. We don't charge – we take the usual one third of any money we recover."

As he is finishing the last sentence, he is pulling a contract out. It's a short contract; one page, three paragraphs, just enough. Deck waves it in his face, so that Van Landel has to take it. He's just had the worst night of his life, he's lucky to be alive, now he has to examine a legal document and make an intelligent decision.

"Can you wait for my wife?" he asks, almost begging.

Are we going to get caught? My nerves are terrible.

"Where is your wife?" he asks.

"She'll be back soon," he says, pain in every word.

"I'll talk to her later, in my office. I need to get a lot of information from her." Deck hands him a pen.

Van Landel quickly signs his name. Deck takes the contract and hands him a business card.

"A couple of things," Deck says. "Don't talk to anyone except your doctor. Insurance people will probably be here today trying to make you sign forms and things. They might even offer you a settlement. Do not sign anything until I read it. You have my number, Rudy Baylor's number is on the back, and you can call us anytime. We'll handle the case together. Any questions? Good," Deck says before he can reply. "Rudy will be back in the morning with some papers. Ask your wife to call us today. It's important that we talk to her." He smiles at Van Landel. It's time to go before he changes his mind. "We're going to get you a lot of money."

We leave quickly. Deck proudly says, "And that is how it is done, Rudy."

"What would you have done if the guy had already had a lawyer?" I ask, beginning to breathe normally again.

"We came here with nothing. We had nothing to lose. You see, Rudy, in law school they don't teach you what you need to know. You were nervous about being there, weren't you?"

"I was. Yes. It's morally wrong to chase ambulances like that."

"Right, but who cares? Better us than the next guy. Another lawyer will try to contact him within the next twenty-four hours. It's simply the way it's done. Competition. There are lots of lawyers out there."

"Will the guy stay with us?"

"Probably. We got to him at the right time. You need to call him in a couple hours, talk to his wife, offer to come back here tonight and discuss the case with them."

"Me? But I'm not sure . . ."

"Look, Rudy, he's our client now. You have the right to visit him and there's nothing anybody can do. Relax."

We drink coffee from plastic cups in a cafe on the third floor. Deck prefers this cafe because it's in a new part of the hospital and very few lawyers know about it.

Part of my new job will be to spend time here looking for possible clients. There are two more hospitals in the area and Deck knows where their cafes are, too.

He advises me to start with St. Peter's because it has the largest emergency room. Nighttime is good, he says, because the patients get bored and, if they can, wheel themselves downstairs for a snack.

Chapter 5   Meeting Kelly

The next morning, Bruiser is at the office early.

"Good work on Van Landel," he says. "Listen to Deck – this could be a nice settlement. The police want to take your statement on the fire. They'll do it here, with me present."

I seem to have no choice. "And if I refuse?" I ask.

"Then they'll probably take you to the station. I suggest you talk to them, then they'll leave you alone."

It's the same two policemen who came to my apartment. The four of us sit around a small table with two tape recorders. They waste time trying to find holes in my story by checking the same, unimportant details. But I'm telling the truth and finally Bruiser gets annoyed and tells them to move forward.

After they leave, Bruiser says he'll talk to their boss and get the file on me closed. "Don't worry – that's the end of it. They don't really think you did it. They just had to question you."

I thank him, and he hands me a tiny phone. "Keep this with

you at all times," he says. "I might need you in a hurry." The tiny thing suddenly becomes much heavier. He'll be able to reach me anytime, anywhere now.

♦

I return to the cafe at St. Peter's to hide and study.

After a while, and to my surprise, I decide that I like it there. The coffee isn't bad, it's quiet, and no one knows me. It's perfect for studying.

The phone rings. It's Bruiser. Any luck? No, I say. Happy fishing, he laughs, and he's gone, probably to Yogi's.

At ten, I am alone in the cafe. I'm studying hard when I hear the tiny cough of a young woman and look up to see a patient in a wheelchair. She is very young and extremely pretty. Her ankle seems to be broken and there are bruises on her face.

An old man in a pink jacket gives her a glass of juice. "There you are, Kelly," he says, gently. "Thirty minutes?"

"Yes, please." He touches her shoulder and leaves.

We are alone, but I try not to stare. When she lifts her glass, I notice the bandages on both wrists.

Although she's pretty, I don't feel like practicing Deck's persuasion skills on her. She looks very sad and I don't want to make it worse. She is wearing a wedding ring. She can't be more than eighteen.

I try to concentrate on the law for at least five uninterrupted minutes, but I notice her wipe her eyes. I realize quickly that her tears are not from the pain of her physical injuries.

Perhaps there was a car wreck and her husband was killed and she was injured. It could be a great case.

I try to concentrate on my book, then I walk across to buy another cup of coffee. When I stop at her table, she slowly raises her beautiful, wet eyes.

I swallow and say, "Is there anything I can do? Are you in pain?"

"No," she says in a whisper. "But thanks."

"Sure," I say. "I'm over there, studying for the bar exam, if you need anything."

"Thanks," she says again.

Minutes pass. I turn a page and look at her at the same time. She's looking at me and my heart misses a beat. I ignore her for as long as I can, then I look up. She's lost again, deep in her suffering. The tears stream down her cheeks.

The kind old man in the pink jacket returns and gently wheels her back to her room. I think about following them, and asking him about her. But I don't.

◆

The next night, at the same table. I listen to the conversations. I ignore a few obvious possible clients and study for hours. My concentration is total.

As ten approaches, I start looking around. I jump whenever a new customer enters the cafe.

About five minutes later, the same elderly man carefully pushes her in. She picks the same table as last night and smiles at me as he gets her orange juice. I think she's wearing a pale red lipstick and a tiny bit of eye make-up. Tonight she is extraordinarily beautiful. Her eyes are clear, shining, free of sadness.

He places her orange juice in front of her, and says the identical words he said last night: "There you are, Kelly. Thirty minutes?"

"Make it forty-five," she says.

I've thought a lot about Kelly today, and I've got a plan. I pretend she's not there for a few minutes and then slowly rise to get another coffee. I stop at her table and say, "You're doing much better tonight."

"I feel much better," she says. "Please sit down. I'm tired of talking to nurses."

"My name's Rudy Baylor. And you're Kelly somebody."

"Kelly Riker. Nice to meet you." She is very pretty from twenty feet, but from this distance she is perfect.

"Why do you come here?" I ask.

"To get out of my room. What about you?"

"I'm studying for the bar exam, and it's a quiet place."

"So you're going to be a lawyer?"

"Sure. I finished law school a few weeks ago, got a job with a firm. I just need to pass the bar exam now. What happened?" I ask, looking at her leg.

"It's my ankle. They put a metal pin in it."

"How did it happen?" This is the obvious next question and I thought it would be easy for her. It's not. She hesitates, and her eyes fill with tears.

"It's a long story," she says, and looks away. "What kind of lawyer do you want to be?"

"I enjoy trial work," I say.

"Representing criminals?"

"Maybe. They have a right to a good defense."

"Murderers?"

"Yeah, but most can't pay for a private lawyer."

"Men who beat their wives?"

"No, never." I'm serious about this, and I'm not sure about her injuries.

The man in the pink coat arrives to take Kelly back to her room. "I enjoyed meeting you," I say.

She smiles and says, "Thanks for the conversation."

"Tomorrow night?" I ask.

"Maybe."

♦

The next day, I give Deck the main details about Kelly Riker. In less than an hour he slides into my office with a proud smile. "Kelly Riker was taken to St. Peter's three days ago at midnight.

24

The neighbors called the police, who found her badly beaten. Her husband, Cliff Riker, was drunk and holding a baseball bat. Kelly gave a short statement. He came home drunk from a baseball game, they fought, he won. She said he struck her twice on the ankle with the bat, and twice in the face with his hand."

"What happened to him?"

"He spent the night in jail, and then his family got him out. He won't go to court, though."

"How do you know?"

"Because it's happened before. Eight months ago the police got the same call. They'd had a similar fight, except she was luckier – he didn't use the bat. Then three months ago he used it and she spent a week at St. Peter's, but she didn't want him to go to jail. It happens a lot."

It takes a moment for me to understand. How can a man beat his wife with a baseball bat? How could Cliff Riker hit such a beautiful face?

"Anything else?"

"No, just don't get too close."

♦

The next time I see Kelly, Cliff is pushing her chair. They quarrel, she starts crying, and then he marches out.

Time passes as Kelly cries silently. Cliff is not coming back, so it's safe to go to her now.

"I'm sorry," she says. "Will you take me to my room?"

We're alone in the elevator. "Are you OK?"

"Yes." She takes my hand. "Thanks. Thanks so much. What did you think of Cliff?"

"You wanted me to see him, didn't you?"

"I guess so."

"He should be shot."

"For a little fight?"

"No, Kelly, any man who beats his wife with a baseball bat needs to be shot."

"How do you know?" she asks.

"Police reports, ambulance reports, hospital records. File for divorce, Kelly."

"I already tried it, but he said he was going to kill me if I didn't stop it. He says he loves me."

♦

The next night, the little old man comes over and says, "Are you Mr. Baylor? Mrs. Riker asked me to give you this."

Dear Rudy:

My doctor said I could go home. Thanks for everything. Say a prayer for us. You are wonderful.

She signed her name and then added:

Please don't call or write, or try to see me. It will only cause trouble.

She knew that I'd be here waiting. I'd never thought that she'd leave but I'm not going to forget her. She needs me, because there's no one else to help her.

I go to a pay phone and find the number. A recorded message tells me her phone's been disconnected.

Chapter 6   The Exam

I'm sitting in my office studying for the bar exam, but it's difficult to concentrate. Why am I falling in love with a married woman? The door suddenly opens and Bruiser rushes in.

"What are you doing?" he demands.

"Studying. It's Friday. The exam starts next Wednesday."

"I just got a call from Leo F. Drummond. He's a partner at Tinley Britt. An excellent trial lawyer – rarely loses."

"I know all about Tinley Britt."

"Well, soon you'll know them even better. They represent Great Benefit. Drummond is the lead lawyer."

Bruiser is talking so fast because he's worried. He's filed a ten million dollar lawsuit against a big company that's represented by a lawyer he really admires.

"What did he say?"

"He tells me the judge will be Harvey Hale, an old friend of his. He thinks a fair verdict is one under ten thousand dollars."

"Sorry I asked."

"So we have Leo F. Drummond and his staff and they have their favorite judge. You've got a lot of work to do."

"Me? What about you?"

"Oh, I'll be around, but this is your case. Remember, they get paid by the hour. The more paper they produce, the more hours they can charge their client for." He laughs and shuts the door.

I suddenly feel very lonely.

◆

Wednesday arrives and the exam papers are passed out at exactly 8 a.m. It's absolutely impossible to tell how well I'm prepared. Booker and I have lunch together, but not a word is spoken about the exam. Dinner is a sandwich, and I'm in bed by nine.

The exam ends at 5 p.m. Friday. We eat pizza, drink a few beers, but are too tired to get drunk. Booker tells me on the way home that the exam has made him physically ill. He's certain that he's failed it. I sleep for twelve hours.

◆

On Monday, there's a note on my desk to see Bruiser.

He pushes a pile of paper across to me. "This is why it's painful to sue big companies. This is Great Benefit's motion to dismiss the Blacks' lawsuit, and it's supported by a sixty-four page document. They'll file every motion they can. They make money, the trial is delayed, you're exhausted. Get busy."

After the third reading, I calm down and start taking notes. I think about how much I hate Great Benefit and what it's done to my client, and I work hard.

Deck has developed a habit of stopping by my office on his way to lunch. Today he tells me he thinks Bruiser is in trouble with a former business partner who has testified against him.

◆

Saturday, a month after I took the bar exam, I get a letter telling me that I passed the bar!

The next morning I shower and go to an expensive coffee bar and read the papers. There's something about the bar exam and a list of people who passed. There I am! It's true. I search for Booker Kane but he's not listed.

I can see him now, helping Charlene dress the children, trying to smile, trying to persuade them both that he'll pass it next time. But I know he's worried about his job.

Booker is a proud man who's always believed he could achieve anything. I would love to drive over there but it wouldn't work. He'll call tomorrow and congratulate me.

◆

Bruiser calls Deck and me into his office. He congratulates me on passing the bar exam before talking about the Van Landel settlement. The Van Landels will be calling in for their share of the hundred thousand dollars later today.

He feels that Deck and I should get something for our work. It's been a quick settlement, and Bruiser has worked on it for less than six hours.

Deck and I are wondering what he did for six hours. His share is a third, $33,000. "I'm going to give you boys a third of that, to be split equally."

"Thanks, Bruiser, that's really generous," I say.

"Yeah, thanks," says Deck. We're both surprised but we're thinking that Bruiser gets $22,000 for six hours work.

But I didn't expect anything and suddenly I feel wealthy.

"Are we ready for tomorrow?" Bruiser asks me. We are going to argue against Great Benefit's motion to dismiss the case.

"I think so," I reply, nervously.

"I might let you handle some of the argument, so be ready. All three of us will go to court. They'll have twenty people there."

♦

Deck and I have lunch at a steak house.

"Very strange," he says. "It's not usual for Bruiser to give money away like this. Something's going to happen. Believe me, I know it is."

"Like what?"

"They're watching him — the police. They'd love to put him out of business."

"Out of business?"

"Yeah, and we'll be caught in the middle. I tell you, Rudy, I'm nervous."

"So what are you saying?"

"We've got to get out . . . now."

I start to ask what he means, but it's obvious. Deck can't work alone and I've passed the bar exam so he needs me.

"We've got money now," says Deck. "We could rent an office, start our own business . . ."

"No — it's too expensive," I reply.

Deck looks at me and smiles. "Hey, I've already found a great place, and it's cheap."

"Now wait a minute, Deck . . ."

"Believe me, we've got to move. I *know* things, Rudy. Things I can't tell you, OK? Bruiser's in big trouble."

I strongly suspect Deck is telling the truth. "Let me sleep on it."

"OK. Let's meet before court tomorrow. In a cafe – we can't talk in our office. Take your files home, and anything else you might want from your office. Now. This afternoon."

◆

I don't sleep much, and it's still dark when I meet Deck.

"Well?" he says.

"Let's try it for a year," I say.

Deck can't hide his excitement. He holds his hand out for me to shake. It's a big moment for him.

"Did you remove all your files?" he whispers.

"Yes. And you?"

"I've been taking stuff out for a week."

At eight, we walk down to our offices, but by eight-fifteen Bruiser has still not arrived. He said he'd be there at eight. Deck and I leave the office at quarter to nine.

"Relax," Deck says, "Bruiser will be in court. And if he's not, you'll do fine."

"Just shut up and drive, Deck."

Bruiser is not outside the courtroom, and as I slowly push open the door and look inside the first thing I don't see is Bruiser. He's not here.

The unpleasant man looking angrily at me must be Judge Harvey Hale. To my left is a group of men who all look the same – short hair, dark suits, white shirts, straight ties, hard faces, nasty little smiles.

"Excuse me, sir, I'm here for the Black case."

"And who are you?"

"My name's Rudy Baylor. I work for Bruiser Stone."

"Where's Mr. Stone?" the judge asks.

"I'm not sure. He was supposed to meet me here."

"Do you want to argue this motion later?"

"No, sir. I'm prepared to argue the motion."

"Are you a lawyer?"

"Well, I just passed the bar."

"But you haven't received your license?"

"No, sir. Next week."

One of the lawyers stands. "For the record, my name is Leo F. Drummond. Of Tinley Britt. We object to this young man arguing the motion without a license." He points at me and I hate him already.

"I've passed the bar exam, Your Honor."

"Mr. Baylor, who will handle this case?"

"I will, Your Honor."

"And Mr. Stone?"

"I can't say. But this is my case. Mr. Stone filed the suit for me, until I passed the bar."

"Very well. Let's continue."

Drummond begins and soon becomes boring. Then it's my turn. I'm nervous, and when I'm finished the judge says, "I'd like to see you both privately."

I wait for Drummond, who is polite. He even tells me I did a good job. The judge is standing behind his desk as we enter.

"Please have a seat." We sit. "I'm really tired of these types of lawsuits. I feel like dismissing the case. Excuse me while I visit the toilet," says Judge Hale, and steps to a small door across the room, locking it loudly.

I'm speechless. Drummond looks at me, all warmth and smiles. "Look, Rudy, I'm a very expensive lawyer from a very expensive firm. With a case like this we calculate the cost of the trial to Great Benefit will be between fifty and seventy-five thousand dollars." He waits for me to say something but I just stare at his tie. "Great Benefit has instructed me to offer you and your clients seventy-five thousand to settle the case."

A dozen wild thoughts race through my mind. Twenty-five

thousand dollars! My fee! I can see it.

But, why is he offering me the money if his friend, Harvey, is ready to dismiss the case? And then I realize it's a routine. Harvey frightens me and then Leo steps in with the gentle touch. How many times have they done this before, here in this office?

"It's a one-time offer, only good for the next forty-eight hours. If you say no, then it's World War III."

He's smooth. His Honor returns from his private little rest room and now it's Leo's turn to excuse himself.

"Not a great lawsuit, I'm afraid," Hale says. "Maybe I can persuade Leo to make an offer of settlement."

"He's just offered me the cost of the defense," I say.

Hale tries to seem surprised. "How much?"

"Seventy-five thousand."

His mouth falls open. "Look, son, you're crazy if you don't take it."

"You think so?" I ask, playing his game.

The door opens and Leo comes back. His Honor stares at Leo and says, "Seventy-five thousand!"

"That's what my client said," Leo explains. I'm sure of two things: First, Hale is serious about dismissing the lawsuit. Second, Drummond is too anxious to settle. I leave the room with Leo's arm around my shoulder.

On the drive back to the office, Deck makes the very good argument that no amount of money will save Donny Ray's life now, so we should take what we can and make things a bit easier for Dot and Buddy.

Bruiser's secretary is crying when we arrive. Nobody has seen Bruiser and she knows something is wrong. I call Yogi's. Prince will know where Bruiser is.

I find out that Prince has gone too. I hope he's safe.

♦

I've got a lot on my mind right now, but I still can't stop thinking about Kelly Riker. I know she's going to get another beating from her husband – it's only a question of time. And the thought of that baseball bat connecting with her beautiful body makes me want to kill him.

Chapter 7   Donny Ray's Statement

Dot seats me at the kitchen table and says Donny Ray is getting weaker and weaker.

"We went to court yesterday for the first time," I tell her. "The insurance company has made an offer to settle the case."

"How much?"

"They calculate they'll pay their lawyers seventy-five thousand dollars to defend the case, so they're offering it now to settle everything."

Dot goes red in the face. "Those bastards think they can shut us up now, right?"

"Yes, that's what they think."

"Donny Ray needed a bone marrow transplant last year. Now it's too late."

"I agree."

Her eyes are red and wet. I was wrong – this mother has not given up. "Just what are we supposed to do with seventy-five thousand dollars? Donny Ray will be dead, and it'll be just me and him." She points at the Fairlane. "I guess you said we'd take it, didn't you?"

"Of course not. I can't settle the case without your permission. We have until tomorrow morning to decide."

"We'd better talk to Donny Ray," she says, and leads me to his bedroom.

Donny Ray gives me a big smile and tries to keep smiling.

Dot holds his hand while he listens carefully.

"Will they go higher?" he asks. Great Benefit has made the jump from zero to seventy-five thousand. Deck and I suspect they may go as high as a hundred thousand, but I won't be so optimistic in front of my clients.

"I doubt it," I say. "But we can try."

"How much will you get?" he asks. I explain how my third comes off the top.

He looks at his mother and says, "That's fifty thousand for you and Dad. You can finish paying for the house. Buy a new car. Put some in the bank for your old age."

"I don't want their money."

Donny Ray touches my arm. "Do you want to settle, Rudy?"

"No, I don't," I say. I look at him, then her. "They wouldn't offer this money if they weren't worried. I want people to know what Great Benefit has done."

I leave them and hope that when I come back tomorrow I won't have to tell them that our case has been dismissed.

◆

Across town, Deck is waiting, smiling proudly.

"What do you think? Four rooms, plus rest room. Not bad," he says. "I thought this would be the reception area – maybe we'll use it for a secretary when we hire one." We step through an open door and into a short hall. "One room on each side. This one here's the largest, so I thought you'd need it."

I step into my new office, and am pleasantly surprised. It's about fifteen feet by fifteen with a window on the street side. It's empty and clean.

"I thought we'd use the other room for conferences. I'll work out of here but I won't make a mess." He's trying hard to please me. Just relax, Deck, I like it.

"Hey, I almost forgot." He turns on the television. It's the noon news report. The first thing we see is our old office. Employees are being allowed to come and go but aren't allowed to remove anything.

The next shot is from outside a club, one of several known for the few clothes worn by its dancers when they are entertaining clients. The police, we learn, are searching for Mr. Stone and Mr. Thomas, who are suspected of a number of criminal activities.

Prince loved cash, I know that much. On my first day at Yogi's, one of the waitresses told me that 80 percent of Prince's income was never reported. Whatever he's done, Prince is my friend and I hope he's safe.

"Run, Bruiser, run," Deck says.

I know Deck's having a hard time controlling his excitement. The idea of having his own office and keeping half the fees without a law license is great for him. The offices will look beautiful in a week.

◆

However, when Deck calls me for the second morning before the sun is up, it's difficult to be nice.

"Have you seen the paper?" he asks.

"I was sleeping."

"Sorry. Bruiser and Prince are on the front page."

"If you want to wake up at four, then fine. But don't call me until seven. No, eight."

"Sorry. But there's more. Guess who died last night?"

"How am I supposed to know? I give up."

"Judge Hale. Fell down dead by his swimming pool."

I try to clear my head. "That's hard to believe."

"Yeah, there's a picture of him. What a bastard."

"How old was he?" I ask. I don't know why.

"Sixty-two. You need to see the paper."

"Yes, I'll do that, Deck. See you later."

35

The paper seems a bit heavier this morning and I'm sure it's because at least half of the stories are about Bruiser Stone and Prince Thomas. They have not been seen. I continue reading and find a very old photo of Judge Hale.

Who will get his job? The local population is half white and half black, but only seven of the top judges are black. Last year, when an old white judge retired, an effort was made to appoint a black judge. It didn't happen.

Many people think that Tyrone Kipler, a Harvard-educated partner at Booker's firm, will be appointed. That's good news since he helped Booker and me with our studies and I have a lot of respect for him.

At exactly nine o'clock I'm at the court house checking the Black v. Great Benefit file. Fortunately, His Honor Hale did not sign an order to dismiss our case before he died.

I call Tinley Britt from a pay phone, and ask for Leo F. Drummond. I express my sorrow at the loss of his friend, and I tell him my clients will not accept his offer. He seems surprised, but has little to say.

"I think that's a mistake, Rudy," he says patiently.

"Maybe, but my clients made the decision, not me."

"Oh, well, then it'll be war," he says sadly. He does not offer more money.

◆

Booker and I have talked twice on the phone since we received the results of the bar exam. As expected, he's not complaining about failing and he's really happy for me. He's already sitting down when I arrive at the cafe, and we order our favorite foods. Charlene and the kids are fine.

He thinks that he may pass the bar anyway, since his score was only one point below the passing mark. He has written to the Board of Law Examiners, who are looking at his exam again. His boss said he'd better pass next time or the firm will have to put someone else in his job.

Booker thinks Tyrone Kipler's appointment is definite. I tell him everything that's happened with the Black case and he laughs when I tell him that it's now sitting in Judge Hale's court waiting for the new judge.

I tell him all about the games Drummond and Hale were playing three days ago when we went to argue the motion. Booker listens closely as I talk of Donny Ray and his twin and the transplant that didn't happen.

"No problem," he says more than once. "If Tyrone gets the appointment, he'll know all about the Black case."

"So you can talk to him?"

"Absolutely. He can't stand Tinley Britt, and he hates insurance companies – he sues them all the time. He'll listen."

Our food arrives. I tell him about my new office, but not my new partner, and he asks a lot of questions about my old office. The whole city is talking about Bruiser and Prince. I tell him everything I know.

◆

The day after Tyrone Kipler is appointed as judge, he calls me into his office, which was Hale's.

Kipler is under forty, speaks softly and looks you straight in the eye. He's extremely bright. I thank him for helping me pass the bar exam.

He says kind things about Harvey Hale, but he's surprised that Hale had so few active cases. He's chosen a few for quick movement and is ready for some action.

"You think this Black case should move quickly?"

"Yes sir. The points are simple. There won't be many witnesses."

"How many statements will you take?"

"Less than ten."

"You'll have trouble with the documents," he says. "I've sued a lot of insurance companies and they never give you all the paperwork. It'll take us some time to get all the documents you're supposed to have."

I like the way he says "us." And there's nothing wrong with it. It is part of his role as judge to help everyone get the evidence they're supposed to have.

"File a motion to have the case heard quickly," he says. "Unless the defense have some very good arguments, you'll get it."

He tells me to call him if I have any questions.

◆

I've got into the habit of calling Donny Ray each afternoon, usually around five. After the first call several weeks ago, Dot mentioned how much it meant to him. We talk about a variety of things, but never his illness or the lawsuit. I tell him about something funny that happened during the day, and I know the calls are an important part of the last days of his life.

He sounds strong this afternoon. He says he's been out of bed and he'd love to go somewhere for a few hours and get away from the house and his parents.

I pick him up at seven and we eat dinner at a little neighborhood cafe. We talk about his childhood – funny stories from the earlier days of Memphis. We laugh a little, probably the first time in months for him, but conversation makes him tired. He hardly touches his food.

Just after dark, we arrive at a park where teams are playing baseball. I help Donny Ray into a folding chair from the trunk of my car, then go and buy him a Coke. He thanks me again and again for bringing him here.

I pay particular attention to one of the players as he walks to the fence and speaks to his girl. Kelly smiles – I can see her eyes shine – and Cliff laughs. He gives her a little kiss and goes back into the game. They appear to be happy. He loves her and wants the guys to see him kiss her.

I should be glad that she appears to be happy and healthy. Maybe he's stopped drinking. Maybe it's time for me to stop thinking about her.

After an hour, Donny Ray is ready for sleep. We drive and talk about his statement. I filed a motion today asking the court to allow me to take a statement from him now that can be used at the trial. He will soon be too weak for two hours of questions from lawyers.

"We'd better do it pretty soon," he says softly.

♦

I was not looking forward to taking Donny Ray's statement in our new offices. They're small and we don't have enough chairs. It would be embarrassing. But on Friday, the day before Donny Ray is supposed to give his statement, Dot tells me that he's too weak to leave the house.

I call Drummond, who says he cannot agree to move the statement from my office to the home of my client – rules are rules, and I'll have to arrange a later date. He's very sorry. He, of course, would like to make it after the funeral.

I call Judge Kipler. Minutes later, Judge Kipler calls Drummond and after just a few minutes the statement is moved to the home of Dot and Buddy Black. Kipler plans to attend. This is extremely unusual but he has his reasons. Donny Ray is seriously ill.

♦

The Black home seems much smaller and hotter. Donny Ray is sitting in bed, more cheerful now. We've talked about this for hours and he says he's ready. Dot is making coffee and washing walls. Buddy has been cleaned, his shirt is white. I can't imagine how Dot managed this. I'm proud of my clients.

Deck has borrowed an old video camera. He looks through the house and tells me quietly that there simply isn't enough room. Judge Kipler arrives, meets everyone, and after a minute says, "Let's take a look outside."

In a corner of the yard is a big, old tree that provides nice shade. "What's wrong with this?" he asks, under the tree. "Let's get some chairs."

Drummond arrives at nine exactly, not a minute early, bringing only two other lawyers with him.

"You'll sit here," His Honor says, pointing to three kitchen chairs.

We seat Donny Ray in a cushioned chair. His breathing is heavy and his face is wet. I politely introduce him to everyone, but he's too weak to shake their hands so he tries his best to smile.

We move the camera directly onto his face. There will be other voices off camera, but his face will be the only one the jury sees.

Kipler asks Donny Ray if he's ready, then instructs the court reporter to start. Donny Ray promises to tell the truth. I ask him his name, address, birthdate, some things about his parents and family. Basic stuff, easy for him and me. He answers slowly and into the camera, just as I've instructed him. He knows every question I'll ask.

Although I didn't tell him to act as sick and weak as possible, he certainly appears to be doing it. Or maybe he only has a few days left to live.

I carefully ask Donny Ray questions about his illness and the treatment he didn't receive. He can't repeat anything his doctor told him and he can't give medical opinions, but other witnesses will, I hope. I finish in twenty minutes.

Leo Drummond introduces himself, for the camera, then explains who he represents and how much he regrets being there. He's not talking to Donny Ray, but to the jury. His voice is sweet. He's a man who cares.

He gently asks whether Donny Ray has ever left this house, even for a week or a month, to live anywhere else. They'd love to show that he left home and so shouldn't be covered by the policy his parents paid for. Donny Ray answers with a polite and sickly, "No, sir."

Did he ever work for a company where health insurance was provided? A few more questions like this are all answered with a soft, "No, sir."

Drummond knows he must be careful. The jury will not like any rough treatment of this young man. He finishes in less than ten minutes.

Dot is quick to wipe her son's face with a wet cloth, as Donny Ray looks at me to see how he did. I smile. Judge Kipler begins carrying chairs back to the house, and Dot and I help Donny Ray to the house. Just before we step into the door, I look to my left. Deck is at the fence, talking to the neighbors and passing out my cards.

♦

I arrive early for my appointment with Dr. Walter Kord and wait for an hour before a nurse comes and takes me to an examination room. A young man of about thirty-five rushes in. "Mr. Baylor?" he says, holding out a hand. "Walter Kord. Let's hurry if we can. I have a lot of patients." I know doctors hate lawyers. I don't blame them.

"We need a statement from you."

"I'm very busy," he says.

"I know. It's not for me, it's for Donny Ray."

"I charge five hundred dollars an hour for testifying."

This doesn't shock me because I expected it. In law school, I heard stories of doctors charging even more. I'm here to beg. "I can't afford that, Dr. Kord. I opened my office six weeks ago and this is the only real case I have."

It's amazing what the truth can do. This guy probably earns a million dollars a year. He hesitates for a second, maybe he thinks of Donny Ray and not being able to help, maybe he feels sorry for me. Who knows?

"I'll send you a bill, OK? Pay when you can."

Chapter 8 Surprises for Drummond

Next it is Dot's turn to make a statement. Judge Kipler wants to be present for this one too. I spent two hours with her yesterday preparing for Drummond's questions. She'll be around to testify at the trial, but this is Drummond's chance to gather information and it will take hours.

Poor Dot's hands are shaking as she sits alone at the end of the table. She's wearing her best cotton blouse, and her best jeans. I explained to her that she did not have to dress up because the video will not be shown to the jury. At trial, however, it will be important for her to wear a dress.

So there are five lawyers and a judge staring at Dot Black as she raises her right hand and promises to tell the truth.

The first hour is spent on family history and Drummond, as usual, is well prepared. Halfway through the third hour we finally get around to the claim. I have prepared a copy of every document connected to the file, including Donny Ray's medical records, and these are in a neat pile on the table. We have no bad documents, but I don't know whether Drummond is so lucky. According to Kipler and Deck, it's not unusual in these cases for the insurance companies to hide things from their own lawyers. In fact, it's quite common, especially when the company has nasty things it would really like to bury.

We start with the policy. The next document is the first letter of denial, then the Stupid Letter. I've told Dot to simply hand this to Drummond without saying anything. It's difficult for her because the letter makes her so angry. Drummond takes it, reads it:

Dear Mrs. Black:

On seven previous occasions, this company has denied your claim in writing. We now deny it for the eighth and final time. You must be stupid, stupid, stupid!

Drummond has spent the last thirty years in courtrooms and he is an excellent actor, but I know immediately that he has never seen this letter. His client didn't include it in the file. His mouth falls slightly open. He reads it a second time. He raises his eyes above the letter and looks at me. I am staring at him, a stare that says, "Caught you, big boy."

Six and a half hours after we started, Kipler says that he's finished.

◆

It's early Sunday morning and I'm riding to the bus station in Deck's car. The weather is clear and beautiful, the first touch of fall in the air. Memphis is lovely in October.

Judge Kipler has set the date of the trial for February 8, and ordered Drummond to make sure that key employees at Great Benefit in Cleveland are available to give statements.

A round-trip plane ticket to Cleveland costs just under seven-hundred dollars. The law firm of Rudy Baylor cannot afford to fly me to Cleveland so I'm going by bus. I'll be in Cleveland by eleven tonight, and the statements from the Great Benefit employees start at nine.

I'm sure that the Tinley Britt lawyers are still sleeping. Later they will have breakfast, read the Sunday paper with their wives, then have a nice lunch. Around five, their wives will drive them to the airport. After an hour in first class, they'll land in Cleveland and

43

be driven to the finest hotel in the city. After a delicious dinner, with drinks and wine, they'll meet in a comfortable conference room and plot against me until late. About the time I check into a cheap hotel, they'll be getting into bed, ready for war.

I, of course, won't be able to sleep.

♦

Around the table are eight enemies in dark suits, white shirts, expensive ties, and black shoes. Eight against one. They look bright-eyed and fresh.

"Now, Rudy, we thought we'd start with the statement of Jack Underhill," says T. Pierce Morehouse, one of the four Tinley Britt lawyers.

"No, I don't think so," I say, nervously.

"Pardon?"

"You heard me. I want to start with Jackie Lemancyzk, the claims handler. But first the file."

"We think you should start with Mr. Underhill."

"I don't care what you think. Shall we call the judge?" Kipler's order clearly states that the six witnesses I've requested should be available at nine this morning, and that I decide in which order to see them.

"Well, we have a problem with Jackie Lemancyzk. She doesn't work here anymore."

I stare at him. "When did she leave?" I ask.

"Late last week."

"We were in court Thursday. Did you know it then?"

"No. She left Saturday."

"Where is she now?"

"She's not an employee. We can't produce her."

"OK, how about Tony Krick, assistant claims examiner?"

"He's gone too."

"How interesting," I say, absolutely amazed. "Has Richard

44

Pellrod, claims examiner, gone too?"

"No, he's here."

"And Russell Krokit?"

"Mr. Krokit left us for another company." Russell Krokit, head of the claims department, wrote the Stupid Letter.

"And Everett Lufkin?"

"No, he's here."

"Where's the file?" Pierce gives me a thick pile of paper. "Give me an hour. Then we'll continue."

"Sure," T. Pierce says. "There's an office there."

I return an hour later. "We need to call the judge."

With T. Pierce on one phone and me on another, I call Kipler. "We've got some problems, Your Honor," I say.

"What kind of problems?"

"Well, of the six witnesses in my notice, three suddenly left the company very late last week." I read him the names.

"How about the file?"

"I've had a look – at least one document is missing."

"What is it?"

"The Stupid Letter."

"Is this true, Pierce?"

"I'm sorry, Your Honor, I don't know. I've gone through the file, but I haven't checked everything."

"Are you guys in the same room?" Kipler asks.

"Yes sir," we both answer.

"Pierce, leave the room. Rudy, stay on the phone."

"OK, Judge, it's just me," I say when Pierce has left.

"What's their mood?" he asks.

"Pretty tense."

"I'm not surprised. By losing witnesses and hiding documents, they've given me the right to order that all statements will be taken down here. Question Underhill only. Ask him everything you can think of but find out what happened to the three missing witnesses. I'll order a hearing for later this week and find out what's going on," he says.

I question Underhill for three hours, then stop. I thought I would have to stay in Cleveland for days, but I leave this place just before two with new documents to examine. These boys will have to come to my town.

The bus ride back to Memphis seems much faster.

◆

On the Thursday, we're in Kipler's courtroom at five-thirty in the afternoon. His Honor picked this time so Leo F. Drummond has to rush over after a long day in court.

"I warned you about the documents, Mr. Drummond. I thought I was rather specific. Now what happened?"

This is probably not Drummond's fault. His client is playing games with him. I *almost* feel sorry for him.

"There's no excuse, Your Honor," he says.

"And when did you first learn that these witnesses don't work for your client anymore?"

"Sunday afternoon."

"Did you try to contact Mr. Baylor?"

"We couldn't find him. We even called the airlines."

They didn't call the bus companies.

"Sit down, Mr. Drummond," His Honor says. "One week from next Monday, we will meet here for the statements of Richard Pellrod, Everett Lufkin, Kermit Aldy, and M. Wilfred Keeley, the company director. They will pay their own travel costs. They will make themselves available to Mr. Baylor and cannot leave until he allows them to. All court costs will be paid by Great Benefit. Copies of all the documents, in order, will be delivered to Mr. Baylor by Wednesday of next week. Great Benefit will also pay Mr. Baylor the cost of his wasted trip to Cleveland. Mr. Baylor, how much is a round-trip plane ticket to Cleveland?"

"Seven hundred dollars."

"Is that first class?"

"No, sir."

"Mr. Drummond, you guys sent four lawyers to Cleveland. Did they fly first class?"

Drummond looks at T. Pierce, who looks like a child caught stealing, then says, "Yes sir, first class."

"I thought so. How much is a first-class ticket?"

"Thirteen hundred."

"How much did you spend on other bills, Mr. Baylor?"

Actually, I spent less than forty dollars. "Around sixty dollars," I say, cheating but not being greedy.

"Then four hours travelling time, at two hundred dollars an hour, that's eight hundred dollars. Any other expenses?"

"Two hundred and fifty to the court reporter."

He writes this down, adds it all up, checks it. "I order the defendant to pay Mr. Baylor two thousand four hundred and ten dollars within five days. If Mr. Baylor does not receive this sum, it will automatically double each day until the check is received. Do you understand, Mr. Drummond?"

I'm smiling. Drummond rises slowly. He's angry. "I object. There is no proof that Mr. Baylor flew first class."

"The trip to Cleveland and back is worth thirteen hundred dollars to your firm, Mr. Drummond. That's what I'm ordering your client to pay."

"Mr. Baylor does not get paid by the hour," he replies.

"Are you saying that his time is not valuable? You'll pay him two hundred an hour. Consider yourself lucky."

I quickly pick up my papers and leave.

♦

For dinner, I eat a bacon sandwich with Dot. Buddy is spending more and more time in his Fairlane. It will only be a few days now before Donny Ray dies, and Buddy's way of dealing with it is to hide out there in the car and drink. He sits with his son for a few minutes each morning, then tries to avoid everybody for the rest of the day.

We talk about the lawsuit, but Dot's lost interest. Six months ago she honestly thought a lawyer, even me, could scare Great Benefit into doing right. There was still hope. Not now.

Dot will always blame herself for Donny Ray's death. She didn't go straight to a lawyer when Great Benefit first denied the claim. Instead, she chose to write the letters herself.

She serves me a cup of coffee and I take it into Donny Ray's room, where he's asleep under the sheets. The only light comes from a small lamp in the corner. The room is still.

Donny Ray has planned the funeral. He wants me to help carry his body.

I pick up the same book I've been reading for two months now, one of the few books in this house. I leave it in the same place and read a few pages on each visit.

I hear a strange voice in the living-room and then a knock on the door. It opens, and I slowly recognize Dr. Kord.

"Just passing by," he says, softly.

"Sit down," I say, pointing to the only other chair. We sit with our backs to the window, our eyes on the dying boy.

"I've been thinking about this trial," Kord says, very quietly. "Any idea when it might happen?"

"February 8."

"Would it be better if I testified in court, instead of recording a statement?"

"Of course."

"Then I'll do it. I won't send a bill."

"That's very generous."

"It's the least I can do. Do you know what my job involves? I diagnose people, then I prepare them for death."

"I guess someone has to do it."

48

"It's not that bad, really. I love my work." He pauses and looks at his patient. "This is a hard one, though. There was treatment available, at a cost. I was willing to give my time and effort, but it's still a two-hundred-thousand dollar operation. No hospital can afford that kind of money."

"It makes you hate the insurance company."

"Yeah, it really does. Let's beat them."

"I'm trying to," I say.

We walk quietly past Donny Ray and say good-bye to Dot, who's sitting out front.

Chapter 9   The Funeral

The phone call I've been afraid of getting finally comes on Sunday morning. It's Dot. She tells me she found him about an hour ago. He went to sleep last night and never woke up.

Her voice is a little weak, but she's managing to control her emotions. We talk for a bit and I realize that my throat is dry and my eyes are wet. I tell her I'm sorry and promise to visit this afternoon. Then I close my eyes and say the last of many prayers for Donny Ray.

I call Judge Kipler with news of the death. The funeral will be tomorrow afternoon at two, which is a problem because the Great Benefit statements are due to start at nine in the morning and continue for most of the week. I'm sure the suits from Cleveland are already in town, probably in Drummond's office right now practicing for the camera.

Kipler tells me to be in court at nine anyway, and he'll handle things from there. I tell him I'm ready.

When I get to the Blacks', the whole neighborhood is there. I tell Dot simply that I am sorry, and she thanks me for coming. I go and sit outside alone.

I'm soon joined by a young man who looks oddly familiar. "I'm Ron Black," he says, sitting. "The twin." He looks strong and healthy.

"Nice to meet you," I say.

"So you're the lawyer." He's not in a talkative mood. His sentences are short and forced, but after a time he tells me that he was ready and willing to give his marrow to save his brother, and that he'd been told by Dr. Kord that he was a perfect match. He's happy to explain this to a jury, and he doesn't ask how much money he might get. After two hours, I'm really tired. I excuse myself and leave.

♦

On Monday, there's a whole crowd of men in dark suits sitting around Leo F. Drummond on the far side of the courtroom. I can imagine how angry the top men from Great Benefit were when they found out that they had to appear here today.

Kipler calls Drummond and me to the front.

"Mr. Drummond, Donny Ray Black died yesterday."

"I'm very sorry," Drummond says.

"The funeral is this afternoon, and that's a problem. Mr. Baylor is taking part in the funeral. In fact, he should be with the family right now. Drummond, have your people here next Monday, same time, same place."

These very important men from Great Benefit will be forced to rearrange their busy lives.

"Why not start tomorrow?" Drummond asks. It's a perfectly good question.

"I run this court and control the trial, Mr. Drummond."

"But Your Honor, these gentlemen have gone to a lot of trouble. It might not be possible next week."

This is exactly what Kipler wants to hear. "Oh, they'll be here, Mr. Drummond. They'll be here Monday morning."

"Well, I think it's unfair, with respect."

"Unfair? We wanted these statements two weeks ago. Your client started playing games."

Kipler is punishing Drummond and Great Benefit. There will be a trial here in a few months, and the judge is telling the famous lawyer that he, His Honor, will rule at the trial.

◆

Behind a small country church, a few miles north of Memphis, Donny Ray Black is laid to rest. I can hear Dot crying softly. I can see Buddy sitting next to Ron. It's a gray, cloudy day, a day for a burial.

◆

We finish with the last statement, from Pellrod, Jackie Lemancyzk's ex-boss, on Wednesday, seven-thirty the following week. After three days of questioning and a thousand pages of statements, the boys from Cleveland are ready to go home.

"Nice job, Rudy," Leo Drummond says in a low voice.

"Thanks."

He breathes deeply. "Look, Rudy, I'd like to discuss settlement possibilities. We feel good about our defense, but this judge is against us."

"How much?" I ask.

"A hundred and fifty thousand."

"My client is dead. His mother buried him last week, and now you expect me to tell her there's some more money on the table. Your timing is terrible."

"What does the lady want? Tell us, Rudy."

"Nothing. He's dead, there's nothing you can do now."

"So why are you going to trial?"

"She wants to show the world what Great Benefit has done, then she wants to destroy it," I say. Drummond is silenced.

◆

Deck is a nervous wreck when I return to the office that evening. His friend Butch, a private detective, is sitting with him. Deck introduces us, refers to Butch as a client, then hands me a note: "Keep talking, not about work."

As we talk about the funeral, Butch quickly unscrews the cap from the phone receiver and points inside to a tiny microphone. "Let's go get some coffee," Deck says.

"Good idea," I say, feeling sick.

Outside, I stop and look at them. "What's going on?"

Deck asked Butch to check our phones. He thought maybe the FBI were listening to us, trying to get information about Prince and Bruiser. There are microphones in all three phones.

"What do we do?"

"Legally, you can remove them," Butch explains. "Or you can just be careful what you say." We go back and search the office for four hours and find nothing. It's only the phones.

After several months in business, our office is beginning to look busier. The front room is crowded with rented tables piled high with documents for the Black case. The phone rings even more now. It's difficult to talk on a phone with a microphone in it.

The mail today is routine, except for two things. First, there is not a single document from Tinley Britt. The second surprise is an invitation to a pre-Christmas sale of gold jewelry in a local mall. Below the store's hours, in a rather lovely handwriting, is the name *Kelly Riker*. No message. Nothing. Just the name.

◆

The jewelry store is one of over a hundred shops in the mall. I enter and walk slowly to the long glass counter where Kelly is helping a customer. She looks up and smiles.

"Can I help you, sir?" I look at her and melt.

We smile at each other. "How are you?" I ask.

"Fine, and you?"

"Can we talk?"

"Not here. There's a cinema down the mall. Buy a ticket for the Eddie Murphy movie. I'll be there soon."

She had it all planned. She knew I'd come.

She arrives a few minutes late. "Are we safe?" I ask her.

"Yeah, he's out with the boys tonight."

"Drinking again?"

"Yes," she says. "But not much."

"I worry about you. I think of you all the time. Do you ever think about me?"

"All the time," she says, and my heart stops. Kelly slides her arm under mine and moves a little closer. Why am I sitting in a dark theater with a married woman?

"Cliff wants me to have a baby."

"Don't do it, Kelly."

"I just wanted to see you, Rudy."

"Either forget about me, or file for divorce."

"I thought you were my friend."

"It's more than friendship, and both of us know it."

"I can't forget about you."

"Then let's file for divorce. I'll help you."

She leans over, gives me a tiny kiss, and leaves.

♦

Deck and Butch have found out that the microphones are not the kind the police or the FBI use. "Somebody else is listening," Deck says over coffee. "But who?"

I make a plan and discuss it with Deck. Deck leaves. Thirty minutes later, he calls to talk about several cases that don't exist. We talk for a few minutes about this and that, then I say, "Guess who wants to settle now?"

"Who?"

"Dot Black."

"Dot Black?" Deck acts surprised.

"Yeah. She said she'd take a hundred and sixty thousand. Since their top offer is one-fifty, she'd win a small victory if they pay more than they want."

"Don't do it, Rudy. This case is worth a fortune."

"I know. But legally, I'm supposed to go to Drummond and try to settle. It's what the client wants."

♦

At five minutes to nine the next morning, the phone rings. It's Drummond. We wired a tape recorder to my phone.

"Rudy, Leo Drummond here," he says. "Rudy, you know my clients want to settle. These guys are important, you know, big-money people with big careers to protect. We'll offer one hundred and seventy-five thousand dollars to settle this thing right now."

"I don't think so."

"Look, Rudy, you need to talk to your client. I think she wants to settle. Call her right now. I'll wait here."

The bastard probably has the microphone wired to his phone. He wants me to call her so he can listen.

"I'll get back to you, Mr. Drummond. Good day."

I hang up and play the tape. Deck and I stare at the recorder. It was Drummond! He put the microphones in.

"I guess we should tell Kipler," I finally say.

"I don't think so," Deck says. "We know that Drummond is responsible because we've just caught him, but we can't prove it. So what's Kipler going to do? Accuse him without proof? Let's save it for the trial. Let's wait for the perfect moment." Both of us smile slowly.

I wait two weeks and call Drummond with the sad news that my client does not want his money. She's acting a bit strange, I say. One day she's afraid of going to trial, the next day she wants her day in court. Right now, she wants to fight.

He doesn't suspect anything. He threatens me by saying that Great Benefit will take the offer back if the Blacks don't settle now. I'm sure this sounds good to the ears listening up in Cleveland.

As for me, I'm slightly surprised at my ability to ignore the money. I'm young and there will be other cases. And I'm sure that Great Benefit is scared and that they are hiding dark secrets. I'm worried, but I'm dreaming of the trial.

◆

Booker and Charlene invite me to Thanksgiving dinner. I get to their house and the first words out of his mouth are, "I passed it." His exam was regraded, his score was raised and now he's a real lawyer!

I tell him that Deck and I have finally made some money. We got a check the other day for a client's insurance claim – twenty-five thousand dollars! The client gets $16,667 and we get exactly $8,333. Deck and I each took $3,000 and left the rest in the firm. I bought a car with my $3,000. Not exactly new, but a big improvement on my old Toyota.

I'm going to spend the Christmas holidays visiting Max Leuberg and other lawyers who have sued Great Benefit.

Chapter 10   An Important Discovery

It's December 23 when I finally arrive in Madison, Wisconsin. I find a small hotel and call Max, who's really happy that I'm in Madison. I've called him about once a month for advice on the Black case, and sent him most of the documents. He knows the trial is six weeks away.

He looks the same – wild hair, jeans, T-shirt. "Any offers to settle?"

"Yeah, several. They're up to a hundred and seventy-five thousand, but my client says no."

"That's unusual, but I'm not surprised. It's one of the best cases I've ever seen, and I've looked at thousands."

I tell him about our phones, and the strong evidence that Drummond is listening to our calls. Then Max and I start work. He wants to beat these people.

"Save the best for last," he says. "Play the tape of Donny Ray testifying just before he died. It's a wonderful picture to leave the jury with."

He slides something across the table to me. "This is Great Benefit's new policy. Sold last month to one of my students. I paid for it. Guess what's not included now?"

"Bone marrow transplants."

"Keep it, and use it in court. I might even have to come and watch this trial."

When Max and I say good-bye at the front door of the law school, I can't thank him enough.

♦

I've talked to four lawyers who've sued Great Benefit. The first three were no help. The fourth, Cooper Jackson, is in Spartanburg, South Carolina. He's not supposed to tell me most of what he tells me. He's settled with Great Benefit, and he and his client signed an agreement never to tell anyone what the details were.

Jackson had a client with a Great Benefit policy who was refused treatment. The claim amounted to eleven thousand dollars. Before they went to court, Great Benefit suddenly wanted a very quiet settlement.

"This is the secret part," he says, obviously enjoying himself. "They paid us the eleven thousand, then threw in another two hundred thousand to make us go away."

"Amazing," I say.

"It's all here," he says, pointing to three large boxes. "Claims are automatically denied, and most people give up. About one in twenty-five will actually go to a lawyer."

"How can you prove this?"

"It's here, in the company manuals."

I look through the manuals. One is for claims, the other for underwriting. At first, they appear identical to the ones I have.

Then I notice something different. In the back of the manual for claims is a Section U. My copy does not have this section, and I begin to understand the way the game is played. The manual for underwriting also has a Section U. When they are read together, the manuals direct each department to deny the claim, then to send the file to the other department with instructions not to pay until they receive further instructions. Those instructions never arrive.

Neither of my manuals has a Section U. The bastards in Cleveland, and possibly their lawyers in Memphis, hid these sections. It is an important discovery.

Cooper says that there are other lawyers suing Great Benefit. We'll keep in touch.

◆

The pre-trial conference is held in the middle of January. We agree that two weeks should be reserved for the trial, though Kipler would like a five-day trial.

"Now, gentlemen, what about the settlement discussions?" asks Judge Kipler. I've told him their latest offer was a hundred and seventy-five thousand. He also knows Dot Black is not interested. "What's your best offer, Mr. Drummond?"

"Well, Your Honor, my clients are willing to offer two hundred thousand dollars to settle."

"Mr. Baylor?"

"Sorry, my client has told me not to settle."

Kipler hands a list to Drummond and me. "Now, these are names and addresses of the possible jurors. Ninety-two. We'll pick the jury a week before the trial, so be ready to go on February 1. You may find out about their backgrounds but any direct contact is a serious offense."

By the time we have to choose the twelve jurors, Drummond will have a nice file on each of these people. The files will be examined by a team of expensive lawyers and psychologists who specialize in juries.

I, on the other hand, have Deck.

♦

I go to the mall at least three times a week now. She's walked by only once so far, but didn't see me.

I sit here tonight watching for her and studying the jurors' information. My model juror is young and black with at least a high school education. But women will be sympathetic to Dot for the loss of her child. The one type of juror I want to avoid is a white male suit like the boys from Cleveland.

Chapter 11   Choosing a Jury

Maybe I'll think of a meaner trick someday, but it's hard to imagine. If Drummond wants to listen to my phone, we'll give him something really interesting.

It's late afternoon. I'm at the office when Deck calls me from the pay phone around the corner.

"Rudy, Deck here. I finally found Dean Goodlow."

Goodlow is a white male, thirty-nine, college education, owns his own business. He's a juror we do not want.

"Where?" I ask him.

"At his office. We were wrong about him. He's not fond of insurance companies. I gave him the facts in our case and he got really mad. He'll make a great juror."

"What a surprise," I say clearly. I want Drummond to hear every word. "How did he feel about talking to you?"

"A little worried. I told him what I told the rest of them. I'm not a lawyer, and if they don't tell anybody about our conversation, then nobody will get in trouble."

"Good. Is Goodlow with us?"

"No doubt. We have to have him."

I pick another person we definitely do not want on the jury. "What about Dermott King?"

"A good man." We go through the same routine with the rest of the names and then Deck says, "What about you?"

"Nathan Butt was a bit surprised to learn that I was one of the lawyers on the case, but he relaxed. He hates insurance companies," I say. I wonder if Drummond's heart is still beating. He knows that he can't do anything except stay quiet and try to avoid the people we talked about.

About fifteen minutes later, the phone rings. A slightly familiar voice says, "Rudy Baylor, please."

"This is Rudy Baylor."

"This is Billy Porter. You came by today. What do you want?" It's actually Deck's friend Butch. Billy Porter is a white male, wears a tie to work and manages a store. We don't want him.

"Yes, well, it's about the trial."

"Is this legal?"

"Of course it's legal, just don't tell anybody. Look, I represent the little old lady whose son was killed by Great Benefit Life Insurance."

"Killed?"

"Yes. The company denied the boy an operation. He died three months ago of leukemia. That's why we sued. We really

59

need your help, Mr. Porter."

I'll bet Leo Drummond doesn't sleep tonight.

♦

The jurors arrive between eight-thirty and nine. For many, it's their first visit to a courtroom, and they're nervous. Dot and I sit alone at the end of our table, facing the jurors. Deck is across the room.

In sharp contrast, the defense table is surrounded by five men in black suits, checking piles of paper which cover the desk. I'm amazed that Drummond does not realize how this looks to the jurors. His client must be guilty, or why would they use five lawyers against only one of me? They clearly have more people and more money than we do. My poor client is weak.

Drummond and his boys refused to speak to me this morning. I could tell that they are shocked and disgusted by my direct contact with the jurors.

Kipler enters the courtroom and everybody rises. Court is opened. He asks which jurors want to be excused and dismisses those, then dismisses some more and we're down to fifty. Kipler goes through a list of questions that he showed to both Drummond and me. This gives us time to watch and study each person.

Then it's my turn. I stand, walk to the bar, smile and say the words that I've practiced a thousand times. "Good morning. My name is Rudy Baylor and I represent the Blacks." After all those questions, they're ready for something different. I look at them warmly, sincerely.

"Now, Judge Kipler has asked a lot of important questions. I have only one more question. Can any of you think of any reason why you shouldn't serve on this jury and hear this case?"

No one says anything. I didn't expect them to. "Thank you," I say with a smile. "The jury looks fine to me, Your Honor."

Drummond is on his feet. He tries to look calm and friendly, but he is burning with anger. He introduces himself and his client, asks a few general questions. Then it starts.

"Now, I'm going to ask you the most important question. Have any of you been contacted about this case?"

It's more of an accusation than a question. The courtroom is perfectly still. "This is very important," he says. "We need to know." There is no trust in his voice. "Let me ask it another way," he says, very coolly. "Did any of you speak with either Mr. Baylor or Mr. Deck Shifflet?"

I jump to my feet, "Objection, Your Honor!"

"I agree. What are you doing, Mr. Drummond?" Kipler shouts.

Drummond says, "Mr. Porter, I'm going to ask you a direct question. I want an honest answer."

"If you ask an honest question, I'll give you an honest answer," Porter says angrily.

"Yes, now, Mr. Porter, did you have a phone conversation last night with Mr. Rudy Baylor?"

I stand, look directly at Drummond but say nothing.

"No, I didn't," Porter says. His face is getting red.

"Are you sure, Mr. Porter?" he demands.

"I certainly am!"

"I think you did," Drummond says. Before I can object and before Kipler can do anything, Billy Porter jumps on Drummond.

"Don't call me a liar, you bastard!" Porter screams and puts his hands around Drummond's throat. Drummond falls. Women scream. One of Drummond's expensive shoes goes flying.

I stay in my seat, thoroughly enjoying the show. After a short break, Drummond makes a formal motion to dismiss the whole group. Kipler refuses, but Billy Porter is excused.

The process of picking jurors continues through the afternoon in Kipler's office. Drummond firmly avoids any of the people

Deck and I mentioned on the phone last night. The result is a jury of my dreams. Six black females, all mothers. Two black males – one a college graduate, one a disabled former truck driver. Three white males, all of whom are sympathetic. One white female, the wife of a wealthy businessman. I couldn't avoid her and I'm not worried. We only need nine of the twelve to agree on a verdict.

The trial starts in a week.

♦

Four days before the trial begins, Deck takes a call at the office from a lawyer in Cleveland. I call him back from the car phone, which doesn't have a microphone in it.

His name is Peter Corsa and he represents a young lady by the name of Jackie Lemancyzk. She went to his office after she was suddenly fired from Great Benefit for no obvious reason.

His client was sexually involved with several of her bosses. Her progress in the company and her pay were based on her willingness. They are filing suit against Great Benefit. I finally ask, "Will she testify?"

I talk to Jackie Lemancyzk for an hour. I promise that her appearance will be a surprise to Great Benefit. She's scared to death of them. I think a surprise would be lovely.

Chapter 12 The Trial

The trial begins. My opening statement is short and goes smoothly. There was a policy, the premiums were paid every week, it covered Donny Ray, he got sick, he was refused treatment and then he died. The purpose of this case is not only to collect money from Great Benefit; it is also to punish them.

Drummond begins by holding up a copy of the policy.

"This is the policy that Mr. and Mrs. Black bought. It doesn't say that Great Benefit has to pay for transplants." The jurors don't like him, but this has their attention. "This policy costs eighteen dollars a week, but they expect my client to pay two hundred thousand dollars for a bone marrow transplant. Now they want the two hundred thousand dollars *and* ten million dollars in punitive damages. I call that greedy." Again and again he repeats himself, saying, "It's simply not in the policy." He decides to push me. The second time he mentions the word "greedy," I object.

Kipler quickly agrees with me.

Dot is our first witness. She describes how awful it was not being able to provide health care for her dying son. Then she reads the letters of denial. They sound worse than I hoped. Denial from claims. Denial by underwriting. All the excuses, letter after letter.

And then, the Stupid Letter. I watch the jurors' faces as Dot reads. They can't believe it. The courtroom is silent.

"Please read it again," I say.

Drummond objects, but Kipler silences him.

Dot reads it again, this time with more feeling. This is exactly where I want to leave Dot. It would be a mistake for Drummond to get rough with her.

He starts with some general questions. Then "Why did you sue Great Benefit for ten million dollars?" He wants to make her look greedy. She expects the question.

"Ten million?" she asks.

"That's right, Mrs. Black. Ten million dollars."

"Is that all?" she asks.

"I beg your pardon."

"I thought it was more than that."

"Is that so?"

"Yeah. Your client has a fortune, and your client killed my son. I wanted to sue for a lot more."

Drummond keeps smiling, and makes one last mistake with Dot Black. "What're you going to do with the money if the jury gives you ten million dollars?"

Imagine trying to answer this in open court, unprepared. Dot, however, is very ready. "Give every penny to the American Leukemia Society. I don't want your rotten money."

"Thank you," Drummond says and sits down quickly. Two of the jurors are openly smiling at his embarrassment.

Next, Ron testifies that he was a perfect match and that he was ready to give his bone marrow to Donny Ray.

Then it's the turn of Dr. Walter Kord. He speaks clearly and explains the disease and treatment so that the jurors can understand. He tells them about the early test that showed Donny Ray had leukemia.

"What does this test cost?"

"Around a thousand dollars."

"And how did Donny Ray pay for it?"

"When he first came to the office, he filled out the normal forms and said he was covered by Great Benefit Life Insurance Company. My staff checked with Great Benefit and found that the policy did exist."

"Did Great Benefit pay?"

"No. We were eventually told that the claim was denied. Mrs. Black has been paying fifty dollars a month."

Dr. Kord repeats the fact that Ron Black was a perfect match for Donny Ray. "If he had had the transplant, it would have worked."

We call Everett Lufkin from Great Benefit to testify. "Who is Jackie Lemancyzk?" I ask him. "Did you know her well?"

"Not really. She was just a claims handler, one of many." Tomorrow she'll testify that their affair lasted three years.

I've explained that the claims manual is the key document that employees refer to. I hand Lufkin the copy I was given by

Drummond before the trial. I ask, "Mr. Lufkin, is this the whole claims manual?"

"Yes."

"Are you certain?"

"Yes."

"I requested a copy from your lawyers and this is what they gave me?"

"Yes."

"Did you personally choose this particular copy of the manual to be sent to me?"

"I did."

I take a deep breath. "Could you open the manual to Section U, please?" He actually takes the manual and goes through it. At this moment, I'm sure he'd sell his children for a Section U. "I don't have a Section U."

I then give him the copy Cooper Jackson gave me.

"Well, Mr. Lufkin, let's talk about the mysterious Section U. Let's explain it to the jury. It went into the manual on January 1, 1991, correct?"

"Yes."

"The year that the Blacks first claimed. Let's read paragraph three." Paragraph three directs the claims handler to immediately deny *every claim* within three days of receiving it. No exceptions. Every claim. If we could stop right now, the jury would give whatever I ask, and they haven't seen Donny Ray yet.

◆

I meet Jackie Lemancyzk's flight and take her to a hotel. We go through the questions I've prepared.

Tuesday morning, we have a few more questions for Lufkin. "Did you suggest to Jackie Lemancyzk that she should leave the company?"

"I did not."

"Did she receive any type of payment when she left?"

"No. She chose to leave."

"Thank you. Your Honor, I've finished with this witness."

Drummond wants to get him out of here. "Your Honor, we're going to keep Mr. Lufkin for later," Drummond says. No surprise – the jury will never see him again.

"Very well. Call your next witness, Mr. Baylor."

I say loudly, "We call Jackie Lemancyzk." Poor Lufkin stops, spins around wild-eyed to the defense table, then walks even faster from the courtroom.

"How long did you work for Great Benefit?" I ask Jackie Lemancyzk.

"Six years."

"And when did your employment end?"

"October 3."

"How did it end?"

"I was fired."

"You didn't choose to leave?"

"No. I was fired."

"Who fired you?"

"Everett Lufkin, Kermit Aldy, Jack Underhall, and others."

I hand her a copy of a letter.

"This is a letter I typed and signed," she says.

"It states that you're leaving for personal reasons."

"The letter is a lie. I was fired so the company could claim that I didn't work there anymore. I was supposed to give a statement about the claim of Donny Ray Black on October 5. On the Saturday before that, I was asked to come to the office for a meeting with Jack Underhall, the man sitting there in the gray suit. He's one of the lawyers at Great Benefit. He told me I was leaving immediately. If I wrote that letter and kept quiet, the company would give me ten thousand dollars."

She bites her lip, struggles for a minute, then is able to

66

continue. "I'm bringing up two children alone, and there are lots of bills, so I had no choice. I wrote the letter, took the cash and signed an agreement never to discuss any of my claims files with anybody."

"Including the Black file?"

"Yes, especially the Black file."

"Then why are you here?"

"I talked to a lawyer. He told me the agreement I signed was illegal."

"Do you have a copy of the agreement?"

"No. Mr. Underhall wouldn't let me keep one. But I'm sure he has the original." I slowly turn and stare at Jack Underhall, so does every other person in the courtroom. His shoes have suddenly become the center of his life.

"Why did you see a lawyer?"

"I needed advice. I was fired for no good reason. But before that, I was forced to have sex with various important people at Great Benefit."

"Anybody we know?"

"Objection, Your Honor," Drummond says. "This has nothing to do with the case."

"Let's see where it goes. Please answer the question, Ms. Lemancyzk."

She takes a deep breath and says, "I had sex with Everett Lufkin for three years. If I was willing to do whatever he wanted, my pay was increased and I progressed in the company. When I got tired of it and stopped, I lost my job and became an ordinary claims handler again. My pay was cut by 20 percent. Then Russell Krokit decided he'd like to have an affair. He forced himself on me, told me that if I didn't accept it, I'd lose my job."

"Both of these men are married?"

"Yes, with families. They went after the young girls in claims. I could give you a lot of names."

I look at Jackie. Her eyes are red now. This is painful for her. The jury is with her, ready to kill for her.

"Let's talk about the Black file," I say. "It was one of your files."

"That's correct. The original claim form from Mrs. Black was given to me. I followed the company policy and I sent her a letter of denial."

"Why?"

"Why? Because all claims were denied at first in 1991."

"All claims?"

"Yes. It was our policy to deny every claim at first, then to go back to the smaller ones later. The big claims were never paid unless a lawyer got involved. It was a one-year trial and it was viewed by management as a wonderful idea. Deny for a year, add up the money saved, subtract the amount spent on quick settlements – leaving a pot of gold."

"How much gold?"

"An extra forty million dollars or so."

"How do you know all this?"

"If you stay in bed long enough with these men, you hear all sorts of garbage. I'm not proud of this, OK?"

"How was the Black claim treated?"

"It was denied like all the rest. But it was a big claim, so Russell Krokit checked everything I did. They soon realized that the policy did allow bone marrow transplants. It became a very serious file for two reasons. First, it was suddenly worth a lot of money. And second, the insured man was going to die."

"So the claims department knew that Donny Ray Black was going to die?"

"Of course. It was clear from his medical records that he would die without the bone marrow transplant."

"Did you show this to anyone?"

"I showed it to Russell Krokit. He showed it to his boss, Everett Lufkin. The decision was made to continue the denial."

"But you knew the claim should be paid?"

"Everybody knew it, but the company was depending on the fact that no more than one out of twenty-five people would talk to a lawyer. They sell these policies to people who are not very educated."

"And when you received a letter from a lawyer?"

"If the claim was under five thousand dollars and it was correct, we paid it immediately and sent a letter of apology. Big claims went to the management. I think they were almost always settled quietly."

"Thank you." I turn to Drummond with a pleasant smile and say, "Your witness." Then I go and sit by Dot, who's in tears. Several of the jurors notice her crying.

Drummond tries to show that Jackie Lemancyzk is testifying because she wants revenge.

"No, I'm here because I know how they cheated thousands of people. This story needs to be told."

After lunch, I call Mr. Wilfred Keeley, the number-one boss at Great Benefit, as a witness. I show him the medical policy Max Leuberg gave me. "Please look at page eleven, Section F, paragraph four, sub-paragraph c, point thirteen. Do you see that?"

The print is so small he has to pull the policy almost to his nose. I look at the jurors. The humor is not missed.

"Got it," he says, finally.

"Good. Now read it, please." He does. "What is the purpose of that section?"

"It explains that we don't pay for transplants."

"Is bone marrow listed as a transplant?"

"Yes. Bone marrow is listed."

I hand him a copy of the Black policy. "What types of transplants are not covered by this policy?"

"Hearts, eyes, all the main ones are listed."

"What about bone marrow?"

"It's not listed."

"So it's not stated that you don't pay for bone marrow transplants?"

"That's correct."

"When was this lawsuit filed, Mr. Keeley?"

"During the middle of last summer. June?"

"Yes, sir," I say. "It was June. Was the language of the policy changed to remove cover for bone marrow transplants after the claim was filed?"

"I don't know."

Our final witness is Donny Ray Black. I sit close to Dot as she wipes her cheek with the backs of her hands. The faces in the jury box are sympathetic. Toward the end, I have a lump in my throat.

We have done all the damage we can to Great Benefit, and I am winning the case. Now we must try not to lose it.

Drummond's first witness is André Weeks, an official in the Department of Insurance for the state of Tennessee. His job is to place the government firmly on the side of the defense.

Drummond hands Weeks the Black policy and they spend half an hour explaining how each policy, *every policy,* has to be examined and passed by the Department of Insurance.

After an extremely boring hour and a half, the jurors begin to lose interest. We stop for a fifteen-minute break, then it's my turn.

I hand him the Black policy and ask a few questions about it. He studies the small print in the policy for a long time as everybody waits. Kipler is smiling. Drummond is angry.

His next witness, Payton Reisky, president of a national insurance group, does even more damage. After Drummond is finished with him, I show him the Stupid Letter. "Mr. Reisky, can you look Mrs. Black in the eye and tell her that her son's claim was handled fairly and properly by Great Benefit?"

It takes him a second or two but he has no choice, "Yes, it certainly was."

70

I have planned to end this way, but I don't expect it to be humorous. One of the jurors actually laughs at his reply. Then the juror behind her starts to laugh. Soon the whole jury box is laughing.

It soon ends, but it is an absolutely wonderful moment.

♦

I go to bed early and fall asleep in seconds.

Less than an hour later, the phone rings. It's an unfamiliar voice, female, young, and very anxious. "I'm a friend of Kelly's," she says, almost in a whisper. "She's in trouble and needs your help."

"What's happened?"

"He came home drunk last night – beat her again."

"Where is she?"

"She's hiding here at my place. After the police left with Cliff, she went to see a doctor. Luckily, nothing's broken. I picked her up."

I get her name and address, then dress in a hurry.

I hardly recognize Kelly. She's been badly beaten. One eye is completely shut. I bend over and kiss her on the top of the head. "Thanks for coming," she says, through damaged lips.

I could kill him.

"Did the police photograph you?" I ask Kelly.

Robin answers, "Yeah, they took a lot of pictures. Show him, Kelly. He's your lawyer, he needs to see."

With Robin's help, Kelly carefully gets to her feet, turns her back to me and lifts her T-shirt above her waist. She is covered in bruises.

"What are you going to do, Kelly?" I ask.

"She has to file for divorce," Robin says. "If she doesn't, he'll kill her."

"Is this true? Are we going to file?"

Kelly says, "Yes, as soon as possible."

"I'll do it tomorrow."

"She can't stay here. Cliff got out of jail this morning and started calling her friends. I told him I knew nothing, but he called back an hour later and threatened me. It won't be long before he finds her. There's a secret safe house for women who are beaten by their husbands, but it costs a hundred dollars a day and she can only stay for a week."

"Is that where you want to go, Kelly?" She says yes.

"Fine. I'll take you tomorrow. This is never going to happen again, understand?"

She whispers, "Promise?"

"I promise. I'll file the divorce in the morning, then I'll come and get you. I'm in the middle of a trial, but I'll get it done."

It's almost 1 a.m. Sleep is impossible so I drive to the office and prepare the divorce papers. In this case, I believe I am really helping to save a life. I fall asleep at my desk.

Deck wakes me at seven. I tell him the story and he reacts badly. "You spent the night working on a stupid divorce? Your closing argument is less than two hours away! Why are you smiling?"

"Great Benefit is going down."

"No, that's not it. You're finally going to get the girl, that's why."

The divorce is on my desk, waiting to be filed. I'll get it sent to Cliff at work.

Chapter 13   The Verdict

The trial has lasted only four days, so the important evidence is still fresh in the jurors' minds. In my closing argument, I repeat the main points of the policy and talk a little bit about bone marrow transplants. I remind them that if Donny Ray had had the transplant, it probably would have saved his life.

I list the hidden documents and the lies that Great Benefit told. The message is plain. In Jackie's words, the management at Great Benefit decided to deny claims for twelve months. It was a trial to see how much extra cash could be made in one year. It was a cold-blooded, greedy decision.

The admitted wealth of Great Benefit is four hundred and fifty million. How do you punish a company as wealthy as this? I ask this question and see the jurors' eyes shining. They can't wait.

I sit next to Dot and wait anxiously to see if Drummond can change defeat to victory.

He begins with a weak apology for the way he behaved when we were choosing the jury. Then he apologizes for Great Benefit, one of the oldest and most respected insurance companies in America. Those letters of denial were awful. His client was wrong. But his client has over six thousand employees – it's impossible to check every letter. No excuses, though. Mistakes were made.

He's trying to soften the jurors. He really doesn't understand why the jury should give Dot Black a percentage of Great Benefit's wealth. It's shocking! How would that help? He has already admitted his client was wrong. The people who were responsible for the unfairness have left the company.

He walks to the board and writes $746 – the Blacks' monthly income. Then he writes $200,000 and multiplies it by 6 percent to get the figure of $12,000. That's $1,000 a month if the money was in the bank.

He then tells the jury what he really wants – to double the Blacks' monthly income. Great Benefit can give them $200,000 and they can put it in the bank!

He's persuasive. I see the jurors considering it.

I hope and pray that they remember Dot's promise to give the money to the American Leukemia Society.

Please do what is fair, he asks, and takes his seat.

But I get the last word. I say, "If the best you can do is two hundred thousand dollars, we don't want it. It's for an operation that will never happen. If you don't believe that Great Benefit deserves to be punished, then they can keep the two hundred thousand and we'll go home." I slowly look into the eyes of each juror as I step along the box. They will not disappoint me.

As Judge Kipler gives them their final instructions, I relax. There are no more witnesses or motions, no more worries about this juror or that. I could sleep for days. This calm lasts for about five minutes, until the jurors leave to begin their discussions. It's almost ten-thirty.

The waiting now begins.

◆

Deck and I file the Riker divorce, then we go straight to Kipler's office. The judge congratulates me on a fine performance and I thank him for the hundredth time. Butch will give Cliff the papers at work.

At noon, lunch is sent into the jury room, and Kipler sends us away until one-thirty. I can't eat. I call Kelly as I drive to Robin's apartment.

Kelly is alone. She's dressed in a loose suit and a pair of Robin's shoes. She has no clothes or anything with her. She walks carefully, in great pain.

"We just filed the divorce papers," I say. "When he gets them he'll go crazy and come after you."

"I hope he does. But he won't, because he's a coward. Men who beat their wives are the lowest kind of cowards. Don't worry. I have a gun."

I take Kelly to the unmarked house on a quiet street. She'll be safe here.

◆

Back at the courthouse, Booker waits with me in the hall until Deck calls my name outside the courtroom doors.

"Just be cool," Booker says, then both of us almost race back to the courtroom. I take a deep breath, step inside and join Dot at our table. Drummond and the other four are in their seats. The jury comes back into the box.

"Has the jury reached a verdict?"

Ben Charnes, the young, black college graduate, says, "We have, Your Honor."

"Please stand and read it."

Charnes clears his throat and reads, "We, the jury, find the defendant, Great Benefit, guilty, and order that they pay two hundred thousand dollars in actual damages." There is a pause. "And punitive damages of fifty million dollars."

The bomb lands and explodes. I'd love to run to the jury box and start kissing feet. I'd love to go and throw my arms around Judge Kipler. But I simply whisper "Congratulations" to my client. She says nothing.

I make a cross in my notebook and write the name Donny Ray Black. I close my eyes and remember my favorite picture of him. I see him sitting on the folding chair at the baseball game, drinking Coke and smiling, just because he's there. My eyes water. He didn't have to die.

Kipler thanks the jury, tells them their little checks will be sent to them and asks them not to discuss the case.

I'm not exactly rich yet. The verdict is so big that there will be a big fight – Great Benefit will not pay easily. I have a lot more work.

Right now, though, I want to go and find a beach.

Kipler closes the trial. I look at Dot and see the tears. She's a hard woman who doesn't cry easily but she is losing control. Someone turns off the lights and we sit in darkness. It's finished.

The last place I want to go is the office. I say good-bye to Deck in front of the courthouse, promise to meet him later. What do you do with sixteen and a half million dollars? I cannot begin to understand this amount of money. I know a dozen things can go wrong. The case could be sent back for a new trial; the verdict could be changed completely.

I know these awful things can happen, but for the moment the money is mine. I dream as the sun sets. Maybe tomorrow I can begin to realize what I've done, but for now, I'm glad to let the poison in my soul go. For almost a year I've lived with a burning hatred of Great Benefit Life. I hope Donny Ray is resting in peace. I hope he knows what happened today.

They've been proved wrong. I don't hate them anymore.

◆

Kelly and I are watching a John Wayne movie, sitting on her bed. She's wearing the same gray suit, no shoes or socks. I can see a mark on her ankle. She's trying to be happy, but she's in such physical pain that it's difficult to have fun. We sit close together, holding hands.

The movie ends and the news comes on. After the usual stories, the announcer says, "History was made today in a Memphis courtroom. A jury returned a verdict of two hundred thousand dollars in actual damages and fifty million in punitive damages against the Great Benefit Life Insurance Company of Cleveland, Ohio, the largest verdict ever in Memphis . . ."

"You won?" she asks.

"I won."

"Fifty million dollars?"

"Yeah. But the money is not in the bank, yet."

"Rudy!"

What can I say? "It's not that difficult. We had a great jury and the facts were clear."

76

"Yeah, right, it happens every day."

"You're right. Right now, I am the greatest!"

"That's better," she says.

Chapter 14   The Last Beating

On Saturday morning the phone rings. "This is Cliff Riker." I start the tape recorder.

"What do you want?"

"Where's my wife?"

"You're lucky she's not dead."

"I'm going to get you, Mr. Big."

"Keep talking, the recorder is on."

The call ends. I call Butch and tell him about my short conversation with Mr. Riker. Butch plans to get Cliff alone, mention the phone call and tell him to stop threatening me or there will be trouble. This is Butch's idea of a good time.

◆

Our date on Saturday is very similar to the one on Friday, except the movie is different. There are a few laughs, a little more touching, but not nearly enough.

She really wants to get out of that gray suit. They wash it for her once a day but she's sick of it. She wants to be pretty again, and she wants her clothes.

She is sure that Cliff will be playing baseball tonight. He never misses a game. So we drive past the baseball field at about seven, then go to the apartment to get her things. I park the car and take a deep breath.

"Are you scared?" she asks.

"Yes." I reach under the car seat and get my gun. We go to her door, the key fits, we're in. "Hurry, Kelly," I say. I put the gun on the kitchen counter. The place is a mess.

I feel like a thief. Every movement makes too much noise. My heart is beating loudly as I carry things from the bedroom to the front door.

"That's enough," I finally say. "Let's get out of here."

There's a slight noise at the door. Someone is trying to get in. She takes a step toward the door, and it flies open. Cliff Riker crashes into the room. "Kelly! I'm home!" he shouts, as he sees her fall over a chair. He swings his baseball bat directly at my head. "You bastard!" he shouts. The bat just misses me. I run at him. "Get the gun!" I shout to Kelly.

He's quick and strong. "I'll kill you!" he shouts, swinging again, missing again. My foot lands perfectly between his legs. He drops the bat. I've got it.

I swing hard and hit him directly across his left ear, and the noise is almost sickening. Bones break. He falls to his hands and knees, then raises his head and starts to get up. My second swing starts at the ceiling and falls with all the force I can find. I bring the bat down with hatred and fear, and it lands solidly across the top of his head.

Then Kelly blocks me. "Stop it, Rudy!"

I stop, look at her and then at Cliff. He's flat on his stomach, making horrible sounds.

"I'm going to kill the bastard, Kelly," I say, breathing heavily, still scared.

"Give me the bat," she says.

"What?"

"Give me the bat and leave."

I'm amazed at how calm she is at this moment. She knows exactly what has to be done.

"What?" I ask, looking at her, looking at him. She takes the bat from my hands.

"Leave. You were not here tonight. I'll call you later."

"OK, OK." I step into the kitchen, pick up the gun. We look at each other. I step outside, close the door quietly behind me, and look around for neighbors. I feel sick.

After ten minutes the first police car arrives. A second quickly follows. Then an ambulance. I sit low in my car in a crowded parking lot, watching it all. Kelly's in there alone and scared and answering a hundred questions, and here I sit, hoping no one sees me. Should I go and save her?

He can't be dead.

I think I'll go back in there.

The fear hits hard. I want them to carry Cliff out and take him to the hospital. I suddenly want him to live. Get up, Cliff, walk out of there.

But Cliff doesn't walk out, he's carried out. The sheet is over his face. He's dead.

I open the door and disappear into the crowd. "He's finally killed her," I hear someone say. Police stream in and out. I listen carefully to what's being said in case anyone saw a stranger leave the apartment.

Minutes later, Kelly comes out with a policeman on each side. She looks tiny, and scared. They place her in the back of a police car, and leave. I walk quickly to my car, and drive to the police station.

I'm taken to a room where Kelly sits alone, waiting to be questioned. I enter with a detective named Smotherton. Kelly is surprised to see me but manages to stay calm. Another officer arrives with a tape recorder. After he turns it on, I say, "I'm Rudy Baylor, lawyer for Kelly Riker. Today is Monday, February 15, 1993. We're at the Central Police Station, Memphis. I'm present because I received a call from my client at about seven forty-five tonight. She had just called 911, and said she thought her husband was dead."

Smotherton starts with basic questions about Kelly and Cliff –

like birth dates, marriage, employment, children. She answers patiently. Her left eye is still black and blue. The bandage is still on her forehead. She's really scared.

She describes the attacks on her in detail and Smotherton sends the other detective to get the records of Cliff's three other beatings. She talks about the baseball bat and the time he broke her ankle with it. She talks about the last beating and the decision to leave and hide, then to file for divorce.

"Why did you go home tonight?" Smotherton asks.

"To get my clothes. I was certain he wouldn't be there."

"Where have you been staying for the past few days?"

"A home for women. Here in Memphis."

"How did you get to your apartment tonight?"

My heart misses a beat, but she's already thought about it. "I drove my car," she says.

"Where is it now?"

"In the parking lot outside my apartment."

"Can we take a look at it?"

"Not until I do," I say, remembering that I'm a lawyer.

"How did you get in the apartment?"

"I used my key."

"What did you do when you got inside?"

"I went to the bedroom and started packing clothes."

"How long were you there before Mr. Riker came home?"

"Ten minutes, maybe."

"What happened then?"

I interrupt at this point, "She's not going to answer that until I've had a chance to talk to her. This interview is now at an end." I push the stop button on the recorder.

Smotherton writes something on a sheet of paper and hands it to me. "This will be treated as a killing but Morgan Wilson's office, which deals with family violence, will consider the circumstances."

"You're keeping her here?"

80

"I have no choice. I can't just let her go."

"I'm going to jail?" Kelly says.

"We have no choice, ma'am." Smotherton says, suddenly much nicer. "Your lawyer can probably get you out tomorrow, but I can't just free you because I want to."

He leaves the room, and I reach across and take her hand. "It's OK, Kelly. I'll get you out as soon as possible."

"How much time could I spend in jail?"

"You have to be found guilty first, and that's not going to happen."

"Promise?"

"I promise. Are you scared?"

She carefully wipes her eyes and thinks for a long time. "He has a large family, and they're all just like him. All heavy-drinking, violent men."

I can't think of anything to say to this. I'm scared of them, too.

"They can't make me go to the funeral, can they?'

"No."

"Good."

They come for her a few minutes later and I watch them lead her down the hall. When they stop at an elevator, Kelly turns toward me. I wave slowly, then she's gone.

Chapter 15   Winners and Losers

Morgan Wilson is a beautiful woman of about forty. She has a firm handshake and a smile that says, "I'm a busy woman. Don't waste my time." Her office is full of files, but very neat and organized. I get tired just looking at all this work to be done. We take our seats, then she realizes.

"The fifty-million-dollar guy?" she asks, with a very different smile now.

"That's me."

"Congratulations," she says. She wants to hear about my good fortune. I give her a description of the trial and what it was like to hear the verdict. Then I tell her why I'm here.

She's a thorough listener, and takes lots of notes. I hand her copies of the new divorce file, the old one, and the records of Cliff's previous visits to the police station. I describe the injuries left by a few of the worst beatings and promise to have Kelly's medical records by the end of the day.

"That poor girl," Morgan says. "How big is she?"

"About five foot five. A hundred and ten pounds."

"How did she beat him to death?"

"She was scared. He was drunk. Somehow she got her hands on the bat."

"Good for her," she says, and I can't believe it. She's completely on Kelly's side.

"I'd love to get her out of jail."

"I need to get the file and read it, but I'll call the clerk and tell him we have no objection. Where's she living?"

"In one of those women's homes, but the poor thing is in jail right now, and she's still black and blue from the last beating."

Morgan waves at all her files. "That's my life."

We agree to meet at nine tomorrow morning.

♦

The next day, at the office, the phone rings. It's Peter Corsa, Jackie Lemancyzk's lawyer in Cleveland.

Corsa congratulates me on the verdict, then tells me some strange stuff is happening at Great Benefit. The FBI arrived at the head offices of Great Benefit in Cleveland this morning and started removing records. Almost all the employees were sent home and told not to come back for two days. A newspaper story says PinnConn, the parent company, has serious financial problems.

There's not much I can say. I killed a man eighteen hours ago, and it's hard to concentrate on other things. He promises to keep me informed.

♦

It seems to take forever, but I finally see Kelly walking toward me, smiling, and I quickly take her to my car. I tell her about threatening calls about her that have been made to the prison. We suspect it's his crazy family. I don't want to discuss last night, and she's not ready for it either.

Peter Corsa calls the office while I'm hiding Kelly. Great Benefit's millions have disappeared. The money was taken out by PinnConn and sent to Europe.

Deck looks like death. We sit in my office for a long time without a word. We haven't discussed it yet, but we both know that we've gone from being paper millionaires to having no money at all.

The phone rings. Deck answers it and listens for a minute. "This guy says he's going to kill you."

"That's not the worst phone call of the day."

"I wouldn't mind getting shot right now," he says.

The sight of Kelly makes me feel better. We eat in her room, with the door locked and my gun on a chair.

There is a short story about Cliff Riker in Wednesday's newspaper, nothing about Great Benefit. Then a message arrives from Peter Corsa's office.

Mr. Wilfred Keeley was arrested yesterday afternoon as he and his wife were waiting to board a flight to London. They claimed to be going away for a quick holiday. They could not, however, produce the name of a hotel anywhere in Europe where they had reservations.

It appears that Great Benefit has been robbed by its parent company over the past two months. The cash went to safe banks all around the world. Anyway, it's gone.

Morgan Wilson has examined Kelly's file and she wants to drop the case. Her boss, Al Vance, isn't so sure.

"It's very simple, Mr. Vance," I say. "If you take it to trial, you'll lose. I'll wave that bat in front of the jury. You guys will look terrible trying to put her in jail."

"He's right, Al," Morgan says. "We couldn't win."

Al needed to hear that from both of us and agrees to dismiss it. Morgan promises to send me a letter this afternoon. I thank them and leave quickly. I almost run through the parking lot to my car.

They're examining a bullet hole in the office window when I arrive. Deck was in the front office, and the bullet missed him by no more than ten feet. His first call was to Butch, who came immediately. Deck tells us he's fine, but his voice is very shaky. Butch says he'll wait just below the window and catch them if they come back. God help the Rikers if they plan another drive-by shooting.

Deck and I decide on a private lunch and we agree on a simple arrangement: Deck gets the files he wants, and I get two thousand dollars, to be paid within ninety days. We agree on the details as we eat, and the business part of the separation is easy. The personal side is not. We both know that Deck has no future.

"I talked to Bruiser last night," Deck says.

"Where is he?"

"The Bahamas."

"Is Prince with him?"

"Yeah."

This is good news, and I'm glad to hear it. I'm sure Deck has known for some time. "So they're safe," I say.

"Yeah. The money's still here, you know."

"How much?"

"Four million. It's what they made from the clubs. It's in Memphis. They want me to take it to Miami."

"Don't do it, Deck."

"It'll take two days and it will make me rich."

"Be careful, Deck."

We shake hands. "You made history, Rudy, you know that?"

"We did it together."

"Yeah, and what do we have to show for it now?"

"Old war stories." Deck's eyes are wet. I watch him drive away.

I go to my bank and take out my savings. Twenty-eight hundred dollars. I hide the bills under the seat of my car.

It's nearly dark when I knock on the Blacks' front door. Dot opens it, and almost smiles when she sees me.

Over coffee, I gently tell her the news about Great Benefit. We probably won't get a penny, ever. I'm not surprised at her reaction. Her eyes shine and her face is happy as she listens.

There appear to be several complicated reasons for Great Benefit's death, but right now it's important for Dot to believe she caused it. She put them out of business. One little woman destroyed those bastards.

She'll go to Donny Ray's grave tomorrow and tell him.

Kelly is waiting anxiously at the home. We sign the paperwork and thank everyone. Then we hold hands and walk quickly to the car, take a deep breath and drive away.

The gun's under the seat, but I've stopped worrying.

"Which direction?" I ask when we get to the highway that circles the city. We laugh at this because it is so wonderful. It doesn't matter where we go!

"I'd like to see the mountains, and snow," she says.

"I think we can find some." She moves closer. It's amazing how little we've planned for this. We didn't know until this morning that she'd be able to leave.

We'll settle in a place where no one can find us. Kelly and I will talk about Cliff's death one of these days, but not anytime soon. We'll pick a small college town because she wants to go to school. She's only twenty. I'd love to teach history in high school. That shouldn't be hard to do. After all, I have seven years of college.

I will not, for any reason, ever be involved with the law. Ever.

ACTIVITIES

Chapters 1–3

Before you read

1 What do you know about the legal system in the United States? In what ways is it similar to the system in your country?

2 Find the words in *italics* in your dictionary. They are all in the story and some have a number of meanings.

   a Which of these words might you find in a book on medicine? Which are common in the insurance industry?

    bone marrow   cover   diagnose   leukemia   policy
    premium   transplant

   b These words are common in legal English. Use forms of the words to complete the sentences from the story.

    bar (n)   *case   client   damages   file* (v)   *(law)suit* (n)
    punitive   settle   sue

    I've ..... a lot of insurance companies.

    I'll have to work with another lawyer, until I pass the ..... exam.

    My ..... want ten million dollars in ....

    Lake ..... the ..... for 2.6 million dollars.

    Let me guess – you ..... the ..... this afternoon.

   c Which of the words below:

    is a form of payment?

    is the end of a marriage?

    is a form of the verb *have* or *be*?

    can refer to a twin?

    refers to someone you don't like?

    ain't   bastard   divorce   fee   identical

After you read

3 Who are these people? What do we know about them?

   a Booker Kane   **c** Prince Thomas

   b Buddy Black   **d** Bruiser Stone

4 Play the roles of Rudy and Dot Black. Use your own words to act out the scene in the club for the elderly.

Student A: You are Dot. Explain your legal problem to Rudy.

Student B: You are Rudy. Ask questions, and promise to help.

Chapters 4–6

Before you read

5 What kind of legal work do you think Bruiser's firm does?

6 Answer the questions. Check the meanings of the words in *italics*.

  a What games are played with a *bat*?

  b What color are *bruises*?

  c If a judge *dismisses* a case, does it continue?

  d Who argues a *motion* in a law court?

  e What possible *verdicts* are there in a murder case?

After you read

7 Who says these lines from the story? Who to? What are they talking about?

  a "You go to the hospitals?"

  b "Keep this with you at all times."

  c "It's a long story."

  d "This is why it's painful to sue big companies."

  e "We've got to get out … now."

  f "Not a great lawsuit, I'm afraid."

8 Imagine you are Mr. Van Landel, lying in your hospital bed. Tell your wife about the lawyers' visit, how you felt and what you agreed.

Chapters 7–9

Before you read

9 Great Benefit has offered the Blacks a settlement. What reasons are there for accepting it? And for refusing it? What do you think the Blacks will decide?

10 What do these words mean in your language?

  evidence   *testify*

After you read

11 Answer these questions.

  a What happens to Prince and Bruiser?

  b What happens to Judge Hale?

  c Why is Judge Kipler sympathetic to Rudy?

  d Why is Donny Ray's statement recorded at home?

  e What is Drummond's reaction to the Stupid Letter?

  f What is the problem with Rudy's phones?

12 Discuss why Judge Kipler decides to make Great Benefit pay for Rudy's trip to Memphis.

Chapters 10–12

Before you read

13 The title of Chapter 10 is "An Important Discovery". Who do you think will make this discovery? What will it be?

14 Find these words in your dictionary. Use each word in a sentence.

  manual (n)   *underwrite*

After you read

15 Why are these important to the story?

  a Section U

  b Drummond's accusations to the jury

  c Jackie Lemancyzk's evidence

  d the Stupid Letter

16 Explain how Rudy and Deck manage to remove from the jury the jurors they do not want.

Chapters 13–15

Before you read

17 What do you think the verdict should be? What do you think it *will* be? Why?

After you read

18 How does the story end for these people?

  a Rudy   **c** Deck

  b Kelly   **d** Prince and Bruiser

Writing

19 Imagine you are Leo F. Drummond. You have just seen the Stupid Letter for the first time, during Dot Black's statement. Write a letter to Great Benefit telling them how you feel about this experience.

20 Write an article for a Memphis newspaper about the Great Benefit case, to appear on the day after the verdict.

21 Compare and contrast the lives and personalities of Rudy Baylor and Deck Shifflet.

22 Imagine that you are either Rudy or Kelly. It is now one year since you left Memphis. Write a letter to either Booker or Robin describing the past year and your life now.

23 Explain the system of private medical insurance that is described in the book. How typical do you think Great Benefit is? How should the system work for both the insurers and their clients?

24 Write a report on the book, including answers to these questions: Where is the action set? When does it take place? Who are the main characters? What are they like? What happens to them? Did you enjoy the book? Would you recommend it to someone else? Why (not)?